Close-up

WORKBOOK A2

Phillip McElmuray

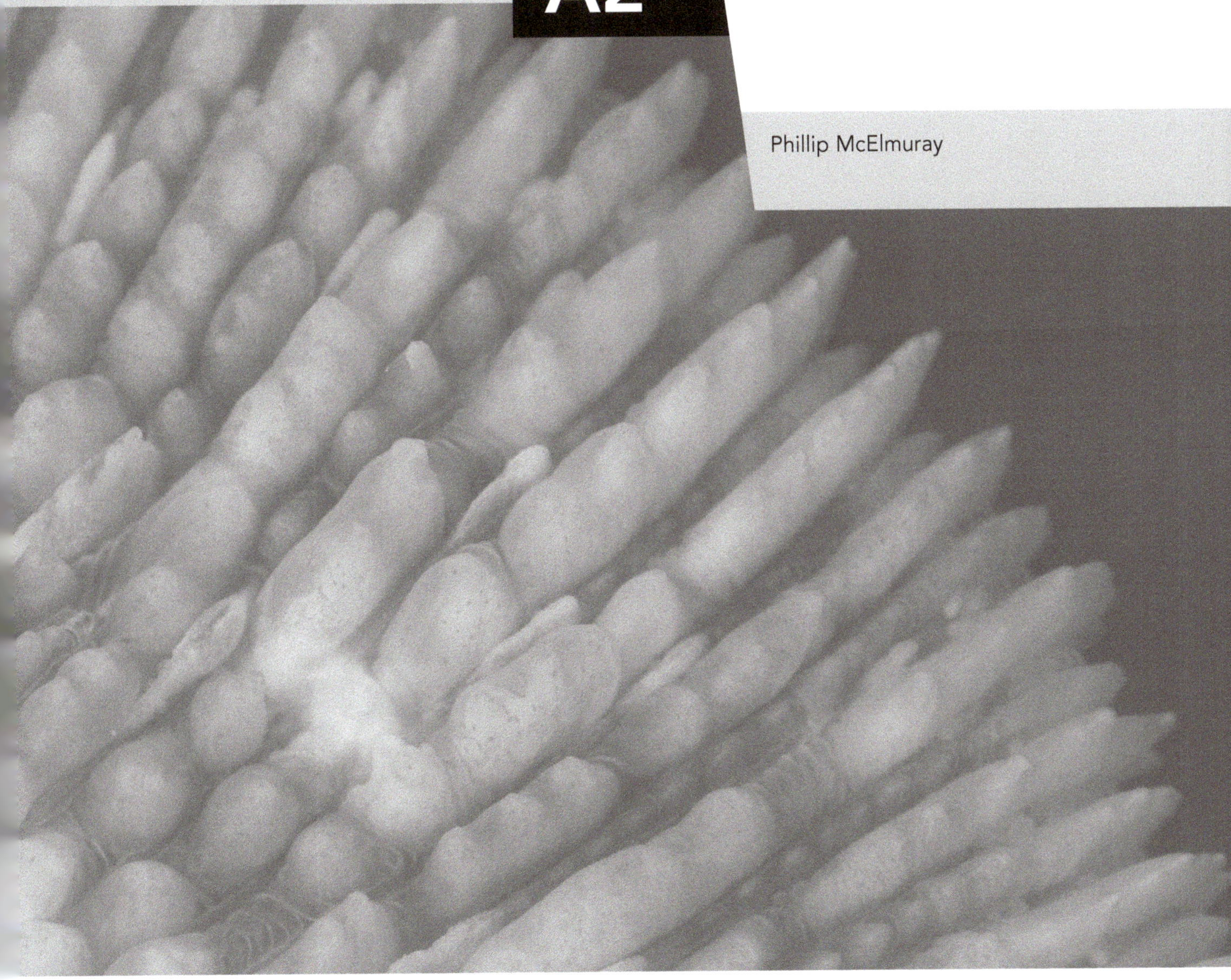

NATIONAL GEOGRAPHIC
LEARNING

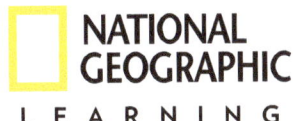

Australia • Brazil • Mexico • Singapore • United Kingdom • United States

Close-up A2 Workbook
Phillip McElmuray

Publisher: Gavin McLean
Editorial Manager: Claire Merchant
Commissioning Editor: Kayleigh Buller
Editor: Nicola Stewart
Head of Production: Celia Jones
Content Project Manager: Melissa Beavis
Manufacturing Manager: Eyvett Davis
Cover Designer: MPS Limited
Text Designer: Wild Apple Design
Compositor: Wild Apple Design

© 2017 National Geographic Learning, a Cengage Learning Company

ALL RIGHTS RESERVED. No part of this work covered by the copyright herein may be reproduced or distributed in any form or by any means, except as permitted by U.S. copyright law, without the prior written permission of the copyright owner.

"National Geographic", "National Geographic Society" and the Yellow Border Design are registered trademarks of the National Geographic Society ® Marcas Registradas

> For product information and technology assistance, contact us at
> **Cengage Learning Customer & Sales Support, cengage.com/contact**
> For permission to use material from this text or product, submit all requests online at **cengage.com/permissions**
> Further permissions questions can be emailed to
> **permissionrequest@cengage.com**

ISBN: 978-1-4080-9689-5

National Geographic Learning
Cheriton House, North Way, Andover, Hampshire, SP10 5BE
United Kingdom

National Geographic Learning, a Cengage Learning Company, has a mission to bring the world to the classroom and the classroom to life. With our English language programs, students learn about their world by experiencing it. Through our partnerships with National Geographic and TED Talks, they develop the language and skills they need to be successful global citizens and leaders.

Locate your local office at **international.cengage.com/region**

Visit National Geographic Learning online at **NGL.Cengage.com/ELT**
Visit our corporate website at **www.cengage.com**

Photo credits: 03 (t) JOHN SCOFIELD/NGC, (b) MACDUFF EVERTON/NGC, 04 AJP/Shutterstock.com, 05 Skreidzeleu/Shutterstock.com, 06 (tl) gdvcom/Shutterstock.com, (tr) Lisa F. Young/Shutterstock.com, (cl) Nadino/Shutterstock.com, (cr) Nadino/Shutterstock.com, (bl) Levranii/Shutterstock.com, (bc) ChiccoDodiFC/Shutterstock.com, (br) MNStudio/Shutterstock.com, 07 Jorg Hackemann/Shutterstock.com, 08 tab62/Shutterstock.com, 10 (t) Ysbrand Cosijn/Shutterstock.com, (c) wavebreakmedia/Shutterstock.com, (b) Nenad Aksic/Shutterstock.com, 11 Dmytriy Aslanian/Shutterstock.com, 12 Monkey Business Images/Shutterstock.com, 13 Monkey Business Images/Shutterstock.com, 14 Ferenc Szelepcsenyi/Shutterstock.com, 18 LuckyImages/Shutterstock.com, 19 gpointstudio/Shutterstock.com, 20 eprom/Shutterstock.com, 21 Monkey Business Images/Shutterstock.com, 24 Reddogs/Shutterstock.com, 25 TonyV3112/Shutterstock.com, 26 Deklofenak/Shutterstock.com, 27 Castleski/Shutterstock.com, 28 (t) Vitalinka/Shutterstock.com, (b) Monkey Business Images/Shutterstock.com, 32 (t) fasphotographic/Shutterstock.com, (c) Tyler Olson/Shutterstock.com, (b) Nativania/Shutterstock.com, 33 CandyBox Images/Shutterstock.com, 34 SuzanneTucker/Shutterstock.com, 35 ThomasZobl/Shutterstock.com, 36 MaximLysenko/Shutterstock.com, 39 (tl) hxdbzxy/Shutterstock.com, (tr) Nagel Photography/Shutterstock.com, (bl) vladimir salman/Shutterstock.com, (br) wavebreakmedia/Shutterstock.com, 40 Mikadun/Shutterstock.com, 41 InnaFelker/Shutterstock.com, 42 BlueOrange Studio/Shutterstock.com, 46 Jack.Q/Shutterstock.com, 47 E.G.Pors/Shutterstock.com, 48 (t) Andy Dean Photography/Shutterstock.com, (b) Zurijeta/Shutterstock.com, 49 Mik Lav/Shutterstock.com, 50 (t) melis/Shutterstock.com, (b) Syda Productions/Shutterstock.com, 52 Bucchi Francesco/Shutterstock.com, 53 BluIz60/Shutterstock.com, 54 Sebastian Rothe/Alamy Stock Photo, 55 (t) muzsy/Shutterstock.com, (c) ChameleonsEye/Shutterstock.com, 56 (t) Fotokostic/Shutterstock.com, (b) Alysta/Shutterstock.com, 60 (tl) E.Glanfield/Shutterstock.com, (tr) Galyna Andrushko/Shutterstock.com, 61 StockCube/Shutterstock.com, 62 (tl) PomInOz/Shutterstock.com, (tr) Jerry Zitterman/Shutterstock.com, (cl) MG image and design/Shutterstock.com, (cr) Kenny/Shutterstock.com, 66 IR Stone/Shutterstock.com, 67 Loredana Cirstea/Shutterstock.com, 68 (t) Arndale/Shutterstock.com, (b) wavebreakmedia/Shutterstock.com, 69 Lightpoet/Shutterstock.com, 70 (t) Spumador/Shutterstock.com, (b) hecke61/Shutterstock.com, 74 S.Borisov/Shutterstock.com, 75 (tl) Smit/Shutterstock.com, (tr) Pedrosala/Shutterstock.com, (cl) John A. Anderson/Shutterstock.com, (cr) Sirapob/Shutterstock.com, (bl) S.Borisov/Shutterstock.com, (br) Jim Lopes/Shutterstock.com, 76 Alexander Yu. Zotov/Shutterstock.com, 77 Radoslaw Lecyk/Shutterstock.com, 78 Victor Maschek/Shutterstock.com, 80 Ivan Kuzmin/Shutterstock.com, 81 Dennis van de Water/Shutterstock.com, 82 (t1) StudioSmart/Shutterstock.com, (t2) Perutskyi Petro/Shutterstock.com, (t3) Chik_77/Shutterstock.com, (t4) Sari ONeal/Shutterstock.com, (t5) kzww/Shutterstock.com, (t6) Jajaladdawan/Shutterstock.com, (t7) Jdm.foto/Shutterstock.com, (t8) Sabine Hortebusch/Shutterstock.com, (c1) AdrianC/Shutterstock.com, (c2) Monkey Business Images/Shutterstock.com, (c3) Jaren Jai Wicklund/Shutterstock.com, (c4) Elena Rostunova/Shutterstock.com, (c5) Pkchai/Shutterstock.com, (c6) Imtmphoto/Shutterstock.com, 83 CatchaSnap/Shutterstock.com, 84 Volodymyr Goinyk/Shutterstock.com.

Design Elements: Nikkytok/Shutterstock.com, Frank Fox/Okapia/Robert Harding Library, Edyta Pawlowska/Shutterstock.com, Odua Images/Shutterstock.com.

Cover image: (front cover) ScubaZoo/Getty Images, (back cover) Karen Gowlett-Holmes/Getty Images

Illustrations: Created by Oxford Designers & Illustrators

Realia: Wild Apple Design

Contents

Unit 1	p 4
Unit 2	p 10
Review 1	p 16
Unit 3	p 18
Unit 4	p 24
Review 2	p 30
Unit 5	p 32
Unit 6	p 38
Review 3	p 44
Unit 7	p 46
Unit 8	p 52
Review 4	p 58
Unit 9	p 60
Unit 10	p 66
Review 5	p 72
Unit 11	p 74
Unit 12	p 80
Review 6	p 86

1 Who Am I?

Reading

A Read the *Exam Reminder*. What do you write next to each paragraph of a text?

_____

B Now complete the *Exam Task*.

Exam Reminder

Reading for main ideas
- Find the most important information in a text to make it easier to understand.
- Look for the main ideas that are in each paragraph.
- Next to each paragraph, write key words to help you remember these ideas.

Malik Chaudry

Malik Chaudry is a brilliant 10-year-old photographer. He lives in Kolkata, India and he takes photographs in his neighbourhood. He's excellent at what he does, and he is already famous for his work. His photography is in galleries in the city centre and he makes money from them.

Malik sees many incredible things where he lives. It's quite crowded and noisy sometimes, but he doesn't mind that much. He knows lots of people in his area, and they are often in his photos. He sometimes takes black-and-white photos, but he really enjoys the colours in his neighbourhood, so he usually takes colour photos.

When Malik isn't taking photos, he hangs out with friends at the local street market. He has three close friends – Dash, Sam and Pavi. They are the same age as him and they like Malik's photos.

Malik's family also like his photos. Malik has a big family. He lives with his mum and dad and his four younger sisters and brothers. They have great fun together, and Malik loves his family very much.

Exam Task

Read the article about a young boy. Are sentences **1–8** 'Right' (**A**) or 'Wrong' (**B**)?
If there is not enough information to answer 'Right' (**A**) or 'Wrong' (**B**), choose 'Doesn't say' (**C**).

1 Malik's hobby is painting. ☐
2 Malik is well-known for what he does. ☐
3 Malik lives in a quiet area. ☐
4 Malik photographs his neighbours. ☐
5 Malik enjoys taking black-and-white photos the most. ☐
6 Dash, Sam and Pavi are in Malik's photos. ☐
7 Dash, Sam and Pavi are 10. ☐
8 Malik is the oldest child in his family. ☐

Vocabulary

A Complete the sentences with the numbers as words.

1 Stephanie has got a big family. Her brother Ricky is 4 _____ and her other brother, Donald, is 6 _____.
2 One of Stephanie's sisters, Ginger, is 12 _____ and the other sister, Alana, is 14 _____.
3 Stephanie is in the middle and she's 10 _____.
4 Stephanie's mother is 42 _____ and her dad is a few years older at 51 _____.
5 Stephanie's mum's parents are 68 _____ and 71 _____.
6 Her dad's mum and dad are 83 _____ and 90 _____.

B Write the dates from the diary in each gap.

My diary

Birthdays

Jake	3/4
Heidi	7/8
Helen	19/2
Mario	24/1
José	8/5
Michele	31/7
Henry	1/3
Beth	12/9

Jake: the _____
Heidi: the _____
Helen: the _____
Mario: the _____
José: the _____
Michele: the _____
Henry: the _____
Beth: the _____

C Complete the sentences with either a country or a nationality.

1 Stephanie's friend Jake is from England. He's _____.
2 Her friend Heidi is Swiss. She's from _____.
3 Helen is from Greece. She's _____.
4 Mario is Italian. He's from _____.
5 José is from Spain. He's _____.
6 Michele is French. She's from _____.
7 Henry is from China. He's _____.
8 Beth is Dutch. She's from the _____.

Young girl waiting for friends in Amsterdam

Who Am I? **1**

D Write the words under the photos.

brother   father   grandma   grandpa   mother   sister

Roberto, _____   Helena, _____

Giorgio, _____   Maria, _____

Stephano, _____   Paulina Graziani   Lisa, _____

E Look at D. Circle the correct words.
1. Roberto and Helena are Paulina's parents / grandparents.
2. Maria is Giorgio's husband / wife.
3. Giorgio is Maria's son / husband.
4. Paulina is Giorgio and Maria's mother / daughter.
5. Stephano is Giorgio and Maria's grandson / son.
6. Stephano, Paulina and Lisa are Roberto and Helena's children / grandchildren.
7. Maria and Giorgio are married / wedding to each other.
8. All of these people are Paulina's family / cousins.

F Read the *Exam Reminder* and complete the *Exam Task*.

Exam Task

Read the descriptions of Paulina's family members. What is the word for each one? The first letter is already there. There is one space for each other letter in the word.

1. Paulina's mother's sister is her **a** _ _ _.
2. Paulina's father's brother is her **u** _ _ _ _.
3. The children of Paulina's aunt are her **c** _ _ _ _ _ _.
4. Graziani is Paulina's **s** _ _ _ _ _ _.
5. The daughters of Paulina's aunt are the same age. They are **t** _ _ _ _.
6. Paulina can call Giorgio **d** _ _ _ _.
7. Paulina can call Maria **m** _ _ _ _.

Exam Reminder

Identifying a set of words
- Look for the vocabulary topic in the instructions. All of the words that you have to find for the task should link to this topic.
- Carefully read the definitions. There is one gap for each letter of the word. This will help you think of the correct word.
- Remember to check your spelling.

1 Who Am I?

Grammar

Present Simple; Adverbs of Frequency; Question Words; Present Continuous

A Read the paragraph. Underline the verbs in the Present Simple form.

My name is Alexis Blezos. I live in Greece. I am 12 years old and I go to Thessaloniki High School. I have two close friends there, Yiannis and Nikos, and we play football together during the lunch break. We sometimes go to the beach at the weekend or we watch TV at my house. Yiannis has a really cool bike. He rides it to school every day. Nikos doesn't have a bike, but he is really funny, so our other schoolmates like him a lot.

B Complete the sentences with the words in brackets.

1 _____ (you / study) every day after school?
2 _____ (Jason / play) the piano?
3 I _____ (not drink) coffee.
4 Mary _____ (not have) many friends.
5 Harry _____ (never / talk) during lunch.
6 They _____ (always / be) late for class.

C Complete the questions with these words.

what   what time   when   where   who   why

1 '_____ is your favourite book?'   'Animal Farm.'
2 '_____ is Ryan?'   'In the library.'
3 '_____ is the new student?'   'His name is Erik.'
4 '_____ do you usually study?'   'At the weekend or in the evening.'
5 '_____ do you take photography lessons?' 'Because I really like it.'
6 '_____ does your music lesson start?'   '6.30 pm.'

D Underline the verbs in the Present Continuous form.

1 Jake is a brilliant musician. He is playing the guitar right now.
2 Francesca likes the Chinese language. She is learning the alphabet at the moment.
3 George is riding his bike to school. His Spanish lesson starts at 8.20 am.
4 Yuri is running for the bus to the city centre. The bus is leaving straight away.
5 I am looking for some new shoes for school. My other shoes are quite old.
6 When are we going to the theatre? The show begins at 2 pm.

E Complete the sentences with the Present Continuous form of the words in brackets.

1 Tom _____ (shop) for a new pair of trousers.
2 I _____ (write) a letter to my friend in South Africa.
3 Why _____ (you / hit) your book with your pencil?
4 Who _____ (make) dinner tonight?
5 Where _____ (Claire / sit) in the audience?
6 Dana and Sam _____ (chat) online to a friend in Mongolia.

F Read the *Exam Reminder* and complete the *Exam Task*.

Exam Task

Read the email about an art lesson.
Choose the best word (**a**, **b** or **c**) for each space.

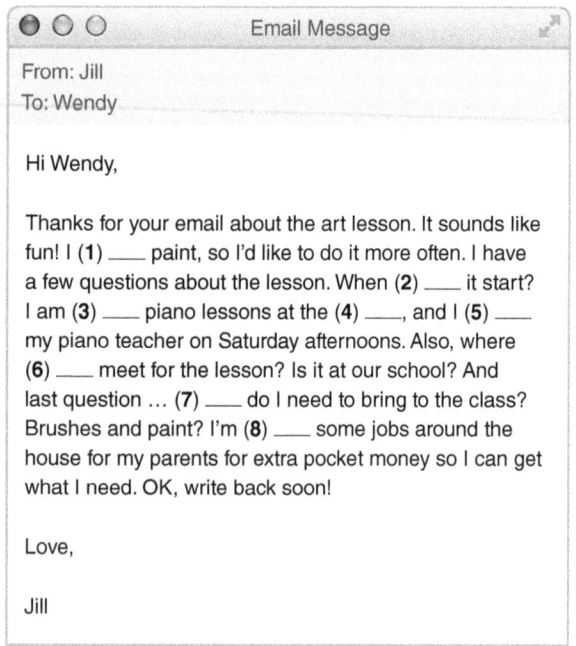

Hi Wendy,

Thanks for your email about the art lesson. It sounds like fun! I (1) ___ paint, so I'd like to do it more often. I have a few questions about the lesson. When (2) ___ it start? I am (3) ___ piano lessons at the (4) ___, and I (5) ___ my piano teacher on Saturday afternoons. Also, where (6) ___ meet for the lesson? Is it at our school? And last question … (7) ___ do I need to bring to the class? Brushes and paint? I'm (8) ___ some jobs around the house for my parents for extra pocket money so I can get what I need. OK, write back soon!

Love,

Jill

Exam Reminder

Choosing the missing words

- Before you start the task, read the whole text to understand the basic meaning.
- Look at each gap and the whole sentence around it. Try to imagine what kind of word would fit in the gap
- Complete the text the second time you read it. Make sure your answers make sense.
- Don't be afraid to guess, and remember to answer all the questions.

1 a often   b hardly ever   c always
2 a do   b is   c does
3 a take   b takes   c taking
4 a moment   b now   c right
5 a always meeting   b always meet   c meet always
6 a do we   b we do   c are we
7 a why   b who   c what
8 a doing   b do   c to do

Listening

A Read the *Exam Reminder*. What can you sometimes find out about the conversation from the instructions?

_____

B 1.1 ▶ Listen and complete the *Exam Task*.

Exam Task

You will hear a teenage girl asking a man about tennis lessons. Listen and complete each question. You will hear the conversation twice.

Sports Club

Place: Stockard Sports Centre

Lessons: tennis

Instructor: (**1**) Kyle _____

Course of (**2**) _____ lessons

Length of lessons: (**3**) _____ hours

Days of lessons: (**4**) every _____ and Thursday evening

Total cost of course: (**5**) £ _____

Exam Reminder

Listening to instructions

- Remember to listen carefully to the instructions you hear before the task starts.
- Find out if the instructions tell you who will speak and where the speakers are.
- Make sure that you understand what to do in the task and how many times you will hear the recording.

C 1.2 ▶ Listen again and check your answers.

1 Who Am I?

Writing: completing a form

A Match the information to the sections of a form.

1. title ☐
2. name ☐
3. date of birth ☐
4. home address ☐
5. email address ☐
6. interests ☐

a Tanya Sanders
b tsanders@mail.com
c painting, reading books
d Ms
e 10 Kings Street, London
f 3rd October, 1992

Learning Reminder

Focusing on accuracy
- Remember that you usually give this information when you complete a form: your title, your first name and surname, your date of birth or age, where you were born, where you live, your phone number, your email address and your hobbies.
- Don't forget that this information must be written in English.

B Read the writing task below and then decide if the statements are true (T) or false (F).

You want to join a sports club. Complete the form.
On the form, you must
- *write all your personal details in pen*
- *explain what sports you are interested in*
- *find out where to buy good sports clothes*

1. You need to write your name and address. ☐
2. It's OK to complete the form in pencil. ☐
3. You need to explain why you like sports. ☐
4. You want to know what clothes to buy. ☐

C Read the example form and correct the mistakes.

Brighton Sports Club

Title (please tick)
Miss ✔ Mr ☐ Ms ☐ Mrs ☐

First name
Hendricks

Surname
John

Date of Birth
2000, 7th May

Street address
18 Montpelier Road

City, Postcode, Country
M27 2AB, UK, Brighton

Interests
I like play all sports, but I especially enjoy playing tennis, so I want to have tennis lessons. I'm also interested in basketball.

Questions
When can I buy good sports clothes?

Remember to write the information in the correct spaces.

Make sure your handwriting is clear.

Remember to use different phrases to talk about what you like.

D Read and complete the *Exam Task* below. Don't forget to use the *Useful Expressions* on page 15 of your Student's Book.

Exam Task

You want to join a social networking site. Complete the form. On the form, you must:
- give your personal information correctly
- answer a question
- write your interests

SocialLife

First name	Country	Why do you want to join SocialLife?
Surname	Nationality	Interests
Age	Email address	

Who Am I? 1

2 Look At Me!

Reading

A Read the *Exam Reminder*. Are the key words in the text always the same as the key words in the questions?

_____

B Now complete the *Exam Task*.

Exam Reminder

Finding the information you need
- Look at the questions and find key words.
- Look for those key words, or words with a similar meaning, in the text.
- Read all the answer choices and choose which is correct.

Look good, be smart!

1

My name's Benjamin, and I'm a TV presenter for a kids' programme. I'm only 18, but the people who make the programme wanted someone young to be the presenter. And they wanted a clever guy who loves fashion, so that's me! I talk about teen news, cool clothes – so teens can look good – and study tips – so teens can be smart! We film the programme when I'm not at school, so I have time to study, too. I love working on the programme, but I want to be smart and finish my education. That's the most important thing.

2

I'm Becky, and I work in a high school, but I'm not a teacher. I'm a guidance counsellor and I help students with problems they have. The teenage years are difficult. They're worried about their appearance, their studies and life in general. I try to make them feel better about themselves and how they look. I tell them that lots of interesting experiences are waiting for them after high school, so study hard and don't worry about having the coolest outfit or a fantastic hairstyle. My best advice is to be yourself, dress how you want and keep on learning!

3

My name's Denise, and I'm studying to be a fashion designer. I'm 19 years old, and I go to my local university. I love fashion, and I used to dress up in my mum's clothes as a child! I like creating traditional designs, but I also love clothing that's colourful and unusual. Fashion is supposed to be fun, isn't it? Some people think some of my designs are weird, but I think they're beautiful. I don't care about being famous, like Donna Karan or Stella McCartney. I just want to make attractive clothes that make people look good!

Exam Task

Read the text about three interesting types of work. For questions 1–7, circle the correct letter, a, b or c.

1 What does Benjamin talk about on his show?
   a clothes
   b his studies
   c films
2 What is most important to Benjamin?
   a school
   b being on TV
   c his looks
3 Who does Becky help?
   a teachers
   b teens
   c small children
4 What advice does Becky give?
   a Wear nice outfits.
   b Keep up with your studies.
   c Look after your hair.
5 What does Denise do?
   a She's a fashion designer.
   b She teaches in a university.
   c She's a student.
6 What does Denise think about fashion?
   a It's a lot of work.
   b It should be fun.
   c It's for children.
7 Why does Denise talk about famous designers?
   a Because she likes their clothes.
   b Because she wants to be like them.
   c To explain what is not important to her.

Vocabulary

A Circle the correct words.

1 Susan has got metal braces / freckles on her teeth.
2 Mark doesn't talk much because he's quite shy / sociable.
3 Maria's got such beautiful blonde / blue eyes.
4 I hate the sun, so that's why I'm always pale / brown.
5 My dad has got a small red eye / moustache.
6 That's a really funny / sociable joke. I'm laughing so much!
7 Michelle has long / short hair that goes down her back.
8 Rachel puts suncream on her hair / skin so she doesn't get burnt.
9 Mario is quite sad / bored because he didn't get on the rugby team.
10 Carole gets good marks at school because she's quite clever / beautiful.
11 I don't like these clothes – they look very great / weird!
12 Oscar is mean / nice. He makes fun of people at school!

B Read the descriptions and complete the words.

1 This word describes a type of hair. w _ _ _
2 You can describe eye and hair colour with this word. b _ _ _ _
3 This describes a happy person. c _ _ _ _ _ _ _
4 This is another word for when someone acts funny or crazy. s _ _ _ _
5 This word describes a type of hair. c _ _ _ _
6 You can describe hair length with this word. s _ _ _ _
7 The words 'pale' and 'a tan' describe this. s _ _ _
8 This is a hair colour. r _ _

Look At Me! 2

C Complete the sentences with the correct form of these words.

annoy beauty friend shock worry

1 'Did you hear that Sarah cheated on the exam?' 'Oh, no! How _____!'
2 That's a _____ dress you're wearing today.
3 I'm _____ about the fact that I don't have a job.
4 My dog looks mean, but she's actually quite _____.
5 Barry gets _____ if you play his video games without asking.

D Complete the adjectives in the sentences.

1 Jake is a very c _ _ _ _ _ teacher who looks after his students.
2 Betty doesn't do much because she's rather l _ _ _.
3 'My computer doesn't work anymore.' 'How a _ _ _ _ _ _ _!'
4 Vicky is close to her daughter. They have a l _ _ _ _ _ relationship.
5 Everyone gets upset when they hear s _ _ _ _ _ _ _ news.
6 Fran is s _ _ _ _ _ of dogs, but she likes horses.

E Circle the correct words.

I really admire my Spanish teacher, Ms Ibanez. She is always kind (1) about / to us in and out of class. We never see her angry (2) about / with anything. She must get angry sometimes, but she never shows it. I know some teachers get annoyed (3) with / to students. It's normal, I suppose. It is probably hard being a teacher sometimes, but Ms Ibanez is very calm. She knows what to do when students are being (4) lazy / friendly and not doing their work. She is good at explaining the Spanish language because she is very (5) traditional / smart. She's very (6) care / caring and always helps students who are worried (7) with / about exams. She takes the time to make them feel better. We have a month of class left, and I'm sad (8) for / about it ending. I know I'll miss Ms Ibanez when the class ends!

F Match the first parts of the sentences 1–6 to the second parts a–f.

1 Is Gemma worried
2 We were really shocked
3 Peter is very sad
4 I didn't do my homework and my dad was so angry
5 Were you annoyed
6 I really like Jenny because she is so kind

a by the theft of your bike.
b to her little brother and sister.
c about his cat at the moment. She's really ill.
d with me. He won't let me go out tonight.
e about the biology exam next week?
f with Dan for breaking your laptop?

G Complete the sentences with one word in each gap.

1 The first people to live in Australia were the _____ Australians, not the Europeans.
2 Anna is really interested in the _____ of Spain – the food, the music, the way of life – so she wants to live there when she's older.
3 My cousin is a great singer, but he doesn't want to be a _____ musician. He just sings for fun and doesn't want to do it for his job.
4 The shamisen is a _____ musical instrument from Japan. It has a very long history and dates from the 16th century.

2 Look At Me!

Grammar

Past Simple; Used to; Past Continuous

A Complete the sentences with the Past Simple form of the verbs in brackets.
1. They _____ (**work**) on the project all night long.
2. I _____ (**buy**) an expensive present for my friend's birthday.
3. She _____ (**think**) about her sister and hoped she likes her new job.
4. We _____ (**go**) to the beach after work.
5. I can't believe you _____ (**eat**) the whole thing!
6. There's no water in the bottle. They _____ (**drink**) it all.

B Make questions from these sentences.
1. You caught the bus in time.
   _____
2. They brought enough food.
   _____
3. They left work at 5 pm.
   _____
4. He was at the doctor's all day.
   _____

C Circle the correct words.
1. My dad **used / use** to live in China, but he left in 2004.
2. I ride a bike to school now, but I used to **took / take** the bus.
3. When did you **see / saw** the new Justin Bieber film?
4. She didn't **got / get** a high mark on her exam.
5. They didn't **used / use** to wear such awful clothes.
6. **Did you / You** use to play in a band as a teenager?

D Complete the sentences with the Past Simple or Past Continuous form of the verbs in brackets.
1. I _____ (**send**) an email when you _____ (**call**).
2. It was a beautiful morning. The birds _____ (**sing**) and the sun _____ (**shine**).
3. The lights _____ (**go**) out when she _____ (**swim**) in the indoor pool.
4. Lisa _____ (**talk**), but sadly, nobody _____ (**listen**).
5. Tom _____ (**run**) to catch the bus when he _____ (**fall**) over.
6. Ms Hanks had a bad day at school. The children _____ (**talk**) a lot in class and the classroom equipment _____ (**not work**) properly.

E Circle the correct words.

Kevin: (1) **Did you enjoy / Were you enjoying** the party on Saturday, Rachel?

Rachel: Yes, I did! It was a great party. When I arrived at 9 pm, the DJ (2) **played / was playing** fantastic music and everyone (3) **was dancing / danced** already. It's a shame you weren't there.

Kevin: I know, but I had homework to do. So while you were having fun, I (4) **studied / was studying** in my room! That's OK, though, because I (5) **was going / went** to the cinema on Sunday and I (6) **was watching / watched** a good film.

Rachel: Oh, what film (7) **were you seeing / did you see**?

Kevin: It was a comedy. I liked it, but it was quite noisy because the audience (8) **used to laugh / was laughing** throughout the whole film.

Rachel: That's good. (9) **Was it showing / Did it show** at the cinema near your house?

Kevin: No, we (10) **drove / were driving** across town to the other cinema. It's a better cinema anyway. The chairs are more comfortable.

Rachel: Well, I'm glad your weekend wasn't completely boring! See you in class later.

Look At Me! **2**

F Read the text and choose the correct answers.

Jenny (1) ____ excited about the visit from her aunt and cousin. She didn't care that the weather wasn't great. It (2) ____ and the sky was grey. But she was happy to be seeing her family, especially her cousin Kathy, because they (3) ____ together a lot when they were small children. They were chatting online together the night before when Kathy (4) ____ her she had a surprise for her. Jenny was excited.

After waiting all morning, Jenny (5) ____ a knock at the door. She ran to open it and saw the surprise that Jenny had. And what (6) ____? It was a very cute puppy, with wavy, dark brown hair and big blue eyes. It was a great day.

1. a used to be b was c was being
2. a was raining b rained c used to rain
3. a were playing b used to play c was playing
4. a used to tell b was telling c told
5. a was hearing b heard c used to hear
6. a was she holding b she was holding c did she hold

Listening

A Read the *Exam Reminder*. How many times will you hear the recording?

_____

B 2.1 Listen and complete the *Exam Task*.

Exam Reminder

Identifying the wrong answers
- Remember to read the questions and options before the recording begins.
- The speakers will often say all the words in the answer options, so listen carefully to find out which ones are wrong.
- Don't choose the answers too quickly, and remember you will hear the conversation again so that you can check your answers.

Exam Task

Listen to Alexander talk to his friend Rocco about a sporting team. For each question, choose the right answer (a, b or c). You will hear the conversation twice.

1. What kind of person is Alexander's favourite player?
   a friendly
   b unkind
   c horrible
2. What is the real colour of Roger's hair?
   a red
   b blonde
   c brown
3. Roger is
   a tall.
   b young.
   c in his thirties.
4. Where is Roger playing today?
   a Lincoln
   b Brighton
   c Leeds
5. The night of the match, Rocco was at
   a the match.
   b home.
   c school.

C 2.2 Listen again and check your answers.

The Harlem Globetrotters team playing a match against the Washington Generals in Budapest, Hungary

2 Look At Me!

Writing: an email

A Complete the sentences with these linking words and phrases.

> and   because   but   for example   so   such as

1 Tom is a good student. _____, he studies every night and he also helps other students.
2 Maggie is a bit shy, _____ she doesn't go out much.
3 I don't think Danielle is a good friend _____ she said mean things about me to Sarah.
4 I usually wear colourful clothes, _____ today I decided to wear black.
5 Michelle likes sporty activities, _____ basketball and tennis.
6 I hang out with Oscar at the weekends _____ we chat online during the week.

Learning Reminder
Writing about personality
- You can write about both good qualities and bad ones when you describe personalities.
- Remember to give examples that support your description and to use the correct linking words, such as *and*, *for example*, *so*, *but*, *that's why* and *because*.

B Read the writing task below and then answer the questions.

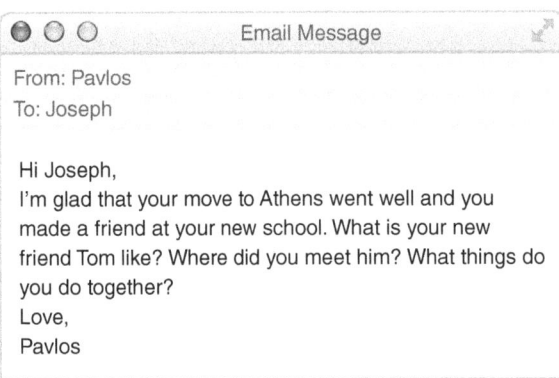

Read the email from your friend, Pavlos.
Write an email to Pavlos and answer the questions.
Write 25–35 words.

1 How many questions do you have to answer? _____
2 Who do you have to write to? _____
3 Should you write more than 35 words? _____

C Read the example email and choose the correct linking words.

There are usually three questions in the email.

> **Email Message**
> From: Joseph
> To: Pavlos
>
> Hi, Pavlos
> Tom is really nice, **(1)** so / because I'm happy we moved here now. He's very funny; **(2)** because / that's why I like him so much. He makes everyone laugh **(3)** so / and he's very kind. We met at school in a maths class, **(4)** but / that's why we didn't speak to each other until lunch break. We often go to the park together **(5)** for example / because we both like playing football.
> Love,
> Joseph

Don't forget to answer all the questions.

D Read and complete the *Exam Task* below. Don't forget to use the *Useful Expressions* on page 27 of your Student's Book.

Exam Task

Read the email from your friend, Sarah.

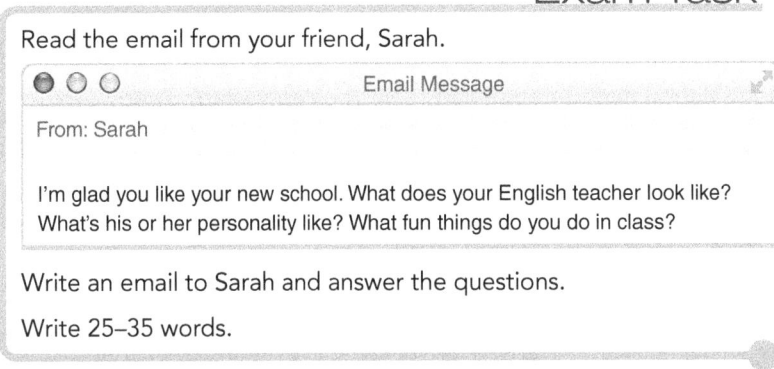

Write an email to Sarah and answer the questions.
Write 25–35 words.

▶ Writing Reference p. 170 in Student's Book

Look At Me! **2**

Review 1

Vocabulary

A Choose the correct answers.

1 I have two ___ who are my aunt's children.
   a sisters   c cousins
   b aunts   d uncles

2 Tom and Sue have a ___ together, and his name is Henry.
   a son   c daughter
   b mother   d twin

3 'When is your birthday, Derrick?'
   'It is in the second month of the year, which is ___.'
   a January   c March
   b February   d April

4 Michaela is Dutch; she was born in ___.
   a France   c the Netherlands
   b England   d Spain

5 'Do you and your sister have the same colour eyes?'
   'No, my sister's eyes are very ___.'
   a tan   c blonde
   b blue   d red

6 Your mum's son is your ___.
   a brother   c sister
   b father   d son

7 'Who is that man?'
   'That's Erica's ___. They've been married for two years.'
   a grandfather c husband
   b brother   d father

8 Your dad's sister is your ___.
   a mum   c uncle
   b sister   d aunt

9 School starts in most countries on the ninth month of the year, which is ___.
   a June   c August
   b July   d September

10 Did you buy any interesting ___ when you were on holiday?
   a souvenirs   c natures
   b street markets d forests

11 My mum's parents have six ___, including my sister, my brother and me.
   a granddaughters c grandparents
   b grandsons   d grandchildren

12 The woman a man is married to is his ___.
   a wife   c mother
   b sister   d daughter

13 It's not very healthy to eat too many ___ between meals.
   a fringes   c braces
   b freckles   d snacks

14 Jake's dad has a thick ___ covering the bottom half of his face.
   a hair   c moustache
   b skin   d beard

15 'I wish I had straight hair like Francesca's.'
   'Her hair isn't straight. It's quite ___.'
   a long   c curly
   b short   d pale

16 Jan has got ___ on her teeth to make them straight.
   a eyes   c braces
   b beards   d freckles

17 My brother's so ___. He talks all the time!
   a shocking   c lazy
   b caring   d annoying

18 I'm worried ___ Heather because she's ill.
   a on   c about
   b to   d with

19 My baby sister is very scared ___ the dark!
   a about   c of
   b to   d for

20 'Bill's quite a ___ person.'
   'I know; he's always telling great jokes.'
   a kind   c funny
   b sociable   d shy

Grammar

B Choose the correct answers.

1. My pen pals Yousef and Amal ___ in Jordan.
   - a is living
   - b living
   - c live
   - d lives

2. 'When do you do your shopping?'
   'I ___ shopping at the weekend.
   - a go often
   - b often to go
   - c goes often
   - d often go

3. ___ do you live in Sweden?
   - a Who
   - b Where
   - c When
   - d What

4. Why ___ wear black to school?
   - a you always
   - b do always
   - c do you always
   - d you do always

5. She ___ late for class.
   - a be never
   - b is never
   - c never is
   - d never be

6. We ___ to a new album at the moment.
   - a listens
   - b 's listening
   - c listen
   - d 're listening

7. I ___ TV right now.
   - a 'm not watching
   - b don't watch
   - c 'm watching not
   - d not watch

8. What book ___ at the moment?
   - a you read
   - b you're reading
   - c do you read
   - d are you reading

9. I ___ in class!
   - a not usually talk
   - b not talking usually
   - c don't usually talk
   - d 'm not usually talk

10. 'Kevin is quite a good student.'
    'I agree. He ___ an exam.'
    - a 's hardly ever failing
    - b hardly ever fails
    - c hardly fails ever
    - d fails hardly ever

11. She ___ her mobile ring this morning.
    - a not hear
    - b don't hear
    - c doesn't hear
    - d didn't hear

12. He ___ for Shelley for over an hour, then he left.
    - a waits
    - b was wait
    - c wait
    - d was waiting

13. 'I think firefighters are great people.'
    'I agree. My dad ___ work as a firefighter.'
    - a was
    - b didn't use
    - c use to
    - d used to

14. 'Where ___ to live before here?'
    'In South Africa and Brazil.'
    - a do they use
    - b they used
    - c did they use
    - d they used to

15. ___ to be on a swimming team when you were young?
    - a You used
    - b You used to
    - c Did you use
    - d Do you use

16. I ___ to the bus stop when the bus suddenly left.
    - a am walking
    - b walk
    - c was walking
    - d walked

17. The wind was blowing, the skies were cloudy and it ___.
    - a were raining
    - b raining
    - c rained
    - d was raining

18. Mum was clearing the table when I ___ the washing up.
    - a were doing
    - b does
    - c was doing
    - d do

19. '___ dinner when I called yesterday?'
    'Yes, but I was glad to hear from you.'
    - a You were having
    - b You had
    - c Did you have
    - d Were you having

20. 'What happened to you last night?'
    'I was sleeping in my bed when I ___ a noise.'
    - a heard
    - b hears
    - c were hearing
    - d was hearing

Review 1   Units 1 & 2   17

3 Let's Get Together

Reading

A Read the *Exam Reminder*. Do you need to match all of the sentences to gaps for the long dialogue?

_____

B Now complete the *Exam Task*.

Exam Reminder

Understanding the context
- To help you choose the right answers, look at the text first and try to work out what the situation is.
- Think about what kind of language people use in that situation.
- When you are matching sentences to gaps in a long dialogue, look at the sentences before and after the gaps to help you find the right answers. Remember that you won't use three of those sentences.

Exam Task

Part 1

Complete the five conversations. Choose **a**, **b** or **c**.

1. Are you cooking spaghetti?
   a No, thanks. I don't like spaghetti.
   b Yes, I ate it yesterday.
   c No, I'm making pizza instead.

2. Thanks for helping me make the cake for the party.
   a No problem.
   b I'd love to.
   c No, thanks.

3. Would you like to go swimming with me?
   a Let's go now!
   b I'm afraid so.
   c That'd be lovely.

4. Neil is coming over later today to watch the game.
   a No, thanks. I'm staying in today.
   b That sounds great. Yes, I'd love to come!
   c Oh, good. What game are you watching?

5. Can you help me paint my room?
   a Of course.
   b It looks great.
   c I already did.

Part 2

Complete the telephone conversation between two friends. What does Elena say to Maria? Choose the correct answer **A–H**. There are three letters you do not need to use.

Maria: Hi, Elena. Can you help me with my new computer?
Elena: (6) ___
Maria: Oh great, thanks! I don't know what's wrong with it, actually.
Elena: (7) ___
Maria: Yes, I can. But some of the programs don't work.
Elena: (8) ___
Maria: My email program and my internet browser. I can't send emails or surf the net.
Elena: (9) ___
Maria: No, it doesn't. Maybe that's the problem.
Elena: (10) ___
Maria: Great, I really appreciate it. You can come in the afternoon if you like.

A Can you turn it on?
B Yes, it could be. I'll have a look later today.
C Which ones do you have a problem with?
D Congratulations on your new computer!
E I can try.
F What's the problem?
G Is it connected to a printer?
H I see. Does it connect to the internet?

C Read the text and decide which conversation from B it relates to.

Technology is changing how people spend time together. Take sport, for example. In the past, people used to go to their friends' houses to watch sport; from international events such as the Olympics or the FIFA World Cup to a local cricket match on a local TV channel. They used to sit in the living room, eat snacks and watch the game together. Now with the internet, people from London to Mumbai to Rio de Janeiro can watch sports events from all over the world easily on their laptops and smartphones. They can watch a greater variety of events, too. But getting together with friends for a game is a bit harder because everyone's so busy, so it's much easier to watch it in your own time. It's a pity. We should make the effort to carry on the old tradition of watching the game with friends at home. Maybe we should turn off the computer and put down the phone more often.

Vocabulary

A Circle the correct words.
1. When Georgia comes through the door, let's throw confetti / presents!
2. You can put the birthday candles / presents for Paul over on that table.
3. Let's hang some pink and blue sparklers / streamers on the walls.
4. Can you help me put these candles / balloons on the cake?
5. Kelly made her friend a chocolate cake / balloon for her birthday.
6. We're going / doing swimming this afternoon. Do you want to join us?
7. Tom's having a barbecue / break in his backyard on Sunday and I'm bringing burgers.
8. We watched a mechanical / spectacular fireworks display on holiday.

B Complete the sentences with one word in each gap.
1. Jill stayed _____ until midnight on Tuesday.
2. It's raining. We have to call _____ the game.
3. Kaye got _____ with three of her friends for coffee.
4. I look _____ to my big brother because he's quite cool.
5. Mary usually hangs _____ with her best friend Karen.
6. I was feeling a bit sick so I stayed _____ for the evening.

C Match the first parts of the sentences 1–8 to the second parts a–g.

1. Most Australians love spending
2. When you get home, can you call Simon
3. I was really looking
4. Ana and her sister didn't use to get
5. Make sure you come home before it gets
6. How was your evening? Did you have
7. Last weekend was fantastic. I had
8. Tom had an argument with his best

a. forward to the party, but I couldn't go because I was ill.
b. too late. I want you to help me make dinner.
c. time in their backyards because the weather is so good there.
d. fun at the party?
e. back? He phoned this morning when you were out.
f. on well with each other, but their relationship is better now.
g. friend yesterday, so he's very upset.
h. a great time at the birthday party on Saturday, then I went to the cinema on Sunday.

Let's Get Together **3** 19

D Complete the words in the sentences.

1. My mum has tea with our neighbour often because she's good c _ _ _ _ _ _ _.
2. Don't be late for the play. It begins at 9 pm s _ _ _ _ _.
3. Kevin sat down and made himself at h _ _ _ _.
4. If you're f _ _ _ on Wednesday evening, come out for a pizza with us.
5. Let's light all the c _ _ _ _ _ _ on the cake before Hank walks in the room.
6. Everyone's looking f _ _ _ _ _ _ to the dance on Saturday!

E Complete the text with these words.

> click   contacted   landline   laptop   online   web

Going (1) _____ is a great way to find old friends. For example, my friend Michael moved away two years ago and we lost touch. I was surfing the internet on my (2) _____ last month when I saw his name on Facebook, so I decided to (3) _____ on it to see his profile. I then (4) _____ him by sending him a message on the site. He wrote back straight away, and soon enough, we were chatting to each other and using a (5) _____ cam to see each other, too. Isn't that cool? I gave him my home number, so he can call my (6) _____ in case I'm not online. I'm glad to have so many ways to communicate with Michael now that I've found him again.

F Read the *Exam Reminder* and complete the *Exam Task*.

Exam Reminder

Identifying collocations

- Words that go together to form a set phrase are called collocations.
- In some tasks, the gaps will often be a missing word from a collocation. Try to think what the word could be before you look at the answer options.
- Look at the words either side of the gap and try to form a phrase with the answer choices. Choose the one that best fits.

Exam Task

Read the sentences about sending letters. Choose the best word (**a**, **b** or **c**) for each answer.

1. Eva likes to send things by ___ from time to time.
   a online   b letter   c post
2. Email is faster, but there's nothing wrong with '___ mail', she says.
   a snail   b slow   c space
3. She doesn't usually send letters because she's got a lot of useful ___ to send emails with easily.
   a devices   b digital   c desktops
4. If she's going to be late, she always ___ her friend a text with her mobile.
   a gives   b sends   c throws
5. But it's nice to write a letter to someone to stay in ___ with them.
   a call   b touch   c text

3 Let's Get Together

Grammar

Present Continuous for future plans & arrangements; Prepositions of time, place, direction & prepositional phrases

A Look at Mark's diary and use the Present Continuous form to write what he's doing this week.

August

Monday
8
Send Bill email

Tuesday
9
Practise the piano

Wednesday
10
Do weekly blog

Thursday
11
Study with Dana

Friday
12
Have pizza with friends

Saturday
13
Visit aunt and uncle

Sunday
14
Sleep late!

Mark is sending Bill an email on Monday. He's _____
_____
_____
_____
_____
_____
_____

B Write questions for these answers using the Present Continuous form of the verbs in brackets.

1 _____
(concert / take place)
'In London.'

2 _____
(you / leave)
'At 10 pm.'

3 _____
(people / go)
'About 20.'

4 _____
(you / meet)
'My friend Sarah.'

C Circle the correct words.

1 I have difficulty studying late at / on / in night.
2 I woke up early because my brother jumped into / in / onto my bed.
3 The room was hot, so Bill walked at / towards / on the open window.
4 Who's the man that just walked onto / on / into the restaurant?
5 What did Ms Smith just write at / on / in the board?
6 How many fish live on / at / in the sea?

D Complete the sentences with these words and any other words you need.

bottom   end   front   middle

1 Good students often sit _____ the class.
2 It's not a good idea to stand _____ a street.
3 You sign your name _____ a letter.
4 My grandma's house is _____ the road.

Let's Get Together 3

E Read the *Exam Reminder* and complete the *Exam Task*.

Exam Reminder

Choosing the correct preposition

- Remember to read the whole text first before you choose any answers.
- When you try to complete a gap, look for a phrase around the gap with one word missing. The missing word is sometimes a preposition.
- Some phrases can be directions, times or places. Try to think of a preposition that works for that phrase in English.
- Once you choose a preposition, say the whole phrase to yourself to check if it sounds right.

Exam Task

Complete the email from a student. Write ONE word for each space.

Hi Simon,
I just want to remind you that we (1) _____ doing our school project (2) _____ 2 pm tomorrow. You remember where my house is, right? It's at the top (3) _____ the hill. My house is (4) _____ the right side of the street. Let's try to finish it this weekend. I have an exam (5) _____ a few days and I want to start preparing early. So we have to stay (6) _____ the house all day and finish the project. We can't go (7) _____ to play football like we did during our last project, OK? Also, did you go (8) _____ Jason's party last weekend? I wanted to go, but it was (9) _____ Sunday, and my family came for a visit that day. It's a shame Jason changed the day of the party (10) _____ Saturday to Sunday.
Jessica

Listening

Exam Reminder

Choosing the correct picture

- When you need to choose pictures for a listening task, look carefully at all the pictures before you listen.
- Try to see the differences between the three pictures for each question.
- Make notes as you listen and use your notes to choose the pictures. Check your answers when you hear the recording the second time.

A Read the *Exam Reminder*. How many pictures are there for each question?

_____

B **3.1** Listen and complete the *Exam Task*.

Exam Task

You will hear five short conversations. You will hear each conversation twice. There is one question for each conversation. For each question, choose the right answer (**a**, **b** or **c**).

1 What is Claire getting for her birthday?

a  b  c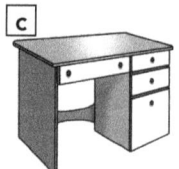

2 What is Tom wearing to the party?

a  b 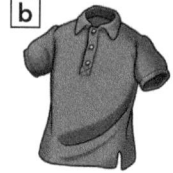 c

3 What time is the exam taking place?

a 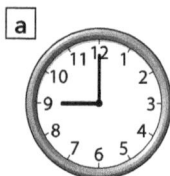 b  c

4 Where is Cindy going to hear music?

a  b  c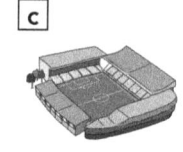

5 When is Paul coming for a visit?

C **3.2** Listen again and check your answers.

3 Let's Get Together

Writing: a poster

A Match the information to these headings.

address   date   email address   event   phone number   time

1 0446548865 _____
2 book club meeting at Dan's _____
3 24 Westville Road _____
4 8.00 pm _____
5 5th December _____
6 dan@gomail.com _____

Learning Reminder

Writing important information
- Remember to include important pieces of information when you write notes or create posters, such as dates, places, times and activities.
- We don't write full sentences when we make posters or write notes. We just write a few words.
- We need to know how to write important information properly.

B Read the email and the notes and then circle the correct answers.

Email Message

Dear Jo,
What a good idea to have a free music party! Stanley Park Leisure Centre is free on Saturday afternoon, so we can have the party there. Can you make a poster to let everyone know? You can use my contact information on it. I'll bring some snacks and drinks.
Speak to you soon!
Jenny

Blackpool Music Party
- 4th of April
- 2 pm – 5 pm
- contact Jenny for information – 5592011 / jgriffin@qmail.com

1 You find out where the party is in the email / notes.
2 You read about someone providing food in the email / notes.
3 You are given Jenny's contact information in the email / notes.

C Read the email and notes in B again and <u>underline</u> the mistakes in the example poster.

There are five notes to complete in this task type.

Find the information in the texts that matches the gaps you need to complete.

Blackpool Music Party!
We're meeting this Saturday, 5th of April at 2 pm and it finishes at 6 pm.
It's in Blackpool Park Leisure Centre. Just look for the signs.
Call Jo on 5592012 for more information, or contact her at jgriffin@qmail.com.
Snacks and drinks for sale

There are two texts in the tasks, so you will need to check both texts.

D Read and complete the *Exam Task* below. Don't forget to use the *Useful Expressions* on page 41 of your Student's Book.

Exam Task

Read the train timetable and the text message. Fill in the information in the poster.

Destination	Leaves	Arrives	Cost of ticket
Eaton Springs	9.00 am	12.20 pm	£16
Newtown	10.30 am	12.30 pm	£12
Colton	9.50 am	1.25 pm	£20

Thanks for sending me the timetable. There are some good ideas for places to go on the class trip on Friday. I think we should go to Newtown. It's cheap and the train journey isn't too long. Can you make a poster with the details?

Join us on Class 4B's summer trip!

We're going to (1) _____ on (2) _____.
We'll get there at (3) _____, so we can spend the whole afternoon there.
The train leaves at (4) _____, so don't be late!

Ticket price: (5) _____

▶ Writing Reference p. 172 in Student's Book

4 A Day in the Life

Reading

A Read the *Exam Reminder*. Where should you look for key words?

_____

B Now complete the *Exam Task*.

Exam Reminder

Finding the right part of the text quickly
- Look for the key words in the questions, then find those words or similar words in the text. Underline the key words in both the questions and the text to help you.
- Does that section of the text answer the question? Compare the text with the question and write your answer. Continue until you answer all of the questions.

My Day with Animals!

Jacie Waters

I'm Jacie, and I'm 15 years old. I work as a volunteer at an animal shelter. I love taking care of animals, and I like having fun with them, too! This is my blog about what I do at the shelter. To begin, here's a typical day for me.

5.30 pm
I get to the shelter. I say 'Hi' to everyone I work with. They're a great group of people, and I look forward to seeing them every day.

5.45 pm
The first thing I do, after saying 'Hi' to the animals, is clean their living areas. It's not my favourite job, but I'm glad to do anything to help the animals. And they're all really friendly!

6.00 pm
Next, I take some dogs out to an outside area. This is a place for them to get some exercise. Of course, I get the most exercise! They run on the grass, and I run with them, too. I get really tired! They also get some snacks, but not too many because they have dinner at 7.00 pm. After a few minutes, I take them back to their living areas and get another group of dogs to take out.

7.00 pm
After the exercise, it's time to eat dinner! Well, not for me! I don't get a break, but I don't really need one. I give food and water to all the dogs, and they're usually quite hungry and thirsty. They love their dinner.

7.30 pm
Finally, I make sure all of the dogs are back in their living areas. It's sad because I hate leaving them. They're very good animals and I hope they find homes soon. I'm always looking for someone to take one home!

Exam Task

Read the blog about Jacie. Are sentences **1–8** 'Right' (**A**) or 'Wrong' (**B**)?
If there is not enough information to answer 'Right' (**A**) or 'Wrong' (**B**), choose 'Doesn't say' (**C**).

1. Jacie talks to everyone at her voluntary job.
2. She really likes cleaning the places where the animals live.
3. The animals are scared of Jacie.
4. Jacie gives the animals a lot of food outside.
5. All the animals get exercise at the same time.
6. Jacie has something to eat before she gets to the shelter.
7. Jacie is sad when she leaves the shelter.
8. Jacie wants to take one of the animals home.

Vocabulary

A Complete the text with these words.

> did   did   dusted   got   had   hung   made   swept   vacuumed

Living on a houseboat is cool, but like ordinary houses, they need to be cleaned! Pieter doesn't like cleaning, but his houseboat was quite dirty. So, on Saturday, he (1) _____ up at 7 am to clean it. After he took a nice warm shower, he (2) _____ his messy bed, went to the kitchen and (3) _____ his breakfast, and started to clean the houseboat. He (4) _____ the carpet in the living room and (5) _____ the furniture after that. Then he (6) _____ the washing up in the kitchen, and he (7) _____ the kitchen floor. He also (8) _____ the washing and then (9) _____ the clothes out to dry. It was a boring way to spend a Saturday, but he was happy that his houseboat was clean.

There are around 2,500 houseboats found along the 165 canals in Amsterdam

B Choose the correct answers.

1. Do you often ___ your clothes before you put them on?
   a brush   b iron   c make
2. The bathroom is so messy. Can you help me ___ it?
   a clean   b wash   c do
3. I'd like to ___ the living room before our friends arrive.
   a make   b take   c tidy
4. The plants are dying! I need to ___ them straight away.
   a do   b wash   c water
5. I'm in a hurry and I don't have much time to ___ dressed.
   a get   b do   c go
6. I always ___ my sister's hair before she goes to school.
   a put   b brush   c make
7. Did you ___ the car yesterday? It looks very nice.
   a wash   b do   c water

A Day in the Life **4** 25

C Complete the text with these words.

> get   home   homework   school   snacks   tired   up

Friday was a busy day! I got (1) _____ at 6.30 am and got ready for school. I took the bus and got to (2) _____ about 8.30 am. We had lessons all morning and then at break I got some (3) _____ from the school shop because I was really hungry. After lunch, we had some more lessons until it was time to go home. I usually walk home, but I was getting (4) _____ so I took the bus again. I got (5) _____ at about 4.15 pm and watched TV for a bit. I got a lot of (6) _____ from the maths teacher, so I did that after dinner. There were some questions I didn't (7) _____, so my dad helped me a bit. After that, I went to the cinema with my friends. The film was brilliant and we had a great time!

D Circle the correct words.

1 Can you eat a whole packet / bar / loaf of chocolate?
2 I can't open this jar / bag / bottle of olives. Will you help me?
3 She gave the children a jar / can / packet of lemonade each.
4 Darla put a packet / carton / tin of tomatoes into the saucepan.
5 How much was that carton / bar / packet of milk?
6 She ate a whole bar / loaf / packet of bread at the weekend!
7 Take a carton / jar / bottle of water with you when you go running.
8 Can you buy a tin / packet / carton of cornflakes at the supermarket, please?

E Complete the dialogue with these words.

> borrow   buying   go   lend   make   pay   save   spend

Gina: Do you (1) _____ a lot of money each month, Hank?
Hank: Not really. I don't (2) _____ shopping often. But when I do, I like (3) _____ clothes and video games. I have to (4) _____ money first because they're expensive.
Gina: Do you (5) _____ a lot of money at your job?
Hank: Not really. My parents sometimes have to (6) _____ me a bit of money to help me (7) _____ my bills.
Gina: I see. Well, if you ever need money, you can always (8) _____ some from me.
Hank: Thanks, Gina. You're a great friend!

F Complete the words in the sentences.

1 Where is the c _ _ _ _ _ _ ? I'd like to pay for these things and leave the shop.
2 The woman looked at her r _ _ _ _ _ _ and saw some items that she didn't buy.
3 Marie, can you push this t _ _ _ _ _ _ round the supermarket for me? I hurt my hand yesterday.
4 There were many people at the t _ _ _ and it took forever to pay.
5 Dan, can you help this c _ _ _ _ _ _ _ find the things she's looking for?
6 There's the jar of jam you want. It's on the bottom s _ _ _ _.
7 Did you do the s _ _ _ _ _ _ _ yesterday? We haven't got any milk.
8 Jenny is r _ _ _ _ _ _ a house with her boyfriend at the moment.

4 A Day in the Life

Grammar

Be going to; Will; Countable / Uncountable Nouns & Quantifiers

A Complete the sentences with *be going to* and the verbs in brackets.

1 I _____ (**do**) the shopping this evening.
2 Ann _____ (**wash**) her sister's hair for her.
3 We _____ (**get**) up at 6 am for the camping trip.
4 _____ (**you / clean**) the kitchen soon?
5 They _____ (**not help**) take out the rubbish.
6 _____ (**he / work**) on his project this weekend?

B Choose the correct answers.

1 I ___ study a lot tomorrow.
   a 'm going   b will   c 'm going to
2 It's cloudy, so it ___ to rain later.
   a 's going to b 's going c will
3 I think I ___ buy this bag. It's quite nice.
   a 'm going to b 'll   c 'm going
4 Don't worry about the exam. You ___ pass it!
   a 're going   b 're going to c 'll
5 It's hot, so I ___ open a window.
   a 'm going to b 'll   c 'm going
6 In ten years, our cities will ___ even larger.
   a going to be b are   c be

C Circle the correct words.

1 'What are your plans for a career?'
   'I'm going to / I'll become an astronaut and fly round the earth.'
2 'I lost my favourite ring.'
   'I'm sure you're going to / you'll find it soon.'
3 'The temperature today will be 35°C.'
   'It'll / It's going to be quite hot in class.'
4 'My phone's ringing, but I can't reach it.'
   'No problem. I'll / I'm going to get it.'
5 'I hope I get into a good university.'
   'Don't worry. I know one will / is going to accept you.'
6 'When does John start his new job?'
   'He's going to / He'll start on the 2nd of January.'

D Find and correct the mistakes in the sentences.

1 Do you have any informations about art classes? _____
2 Traffic is bad here because everyone drives car to work. _____
3 Mum, I need some money to buy new shoe. _____
4 There is absolutely no foods in any of these cupboards. _____
5 Her house has sixteen rooms, but hardly any furnitures. _____
6 Hank plays video game after he finishes his homework. _____
7 There were six child at the party, but only five chairs. _____
8 Maths and science are my two favourite subject. _____

A Day in the Life **4**

E Complete the text with these words.

any few little lot many much some

Ivana lives in Serbia. She's got quite a big family, with (1) _____ brothers and sisters, five in total. They live with their mum and dad in a large house with a (2) _____ of rooms. There are only four bedrooms, though, so Ivana has to share a room. She doesn't have (3) _____ time to herself, but there are (4) _____ good things about having a big family. She doesn't have to do all the chores. In fact, because she's ten, she only does a (5) _____ cleaning in the house. She makes her bed and she picks up a (6) _____ clothes off the floor. She helps do the washing up, but she doesn't have to wash (7) _____ clothes. Her mum does that. For the other chores, everyone does their share of work!

Listening

A Read the *Exam Reminder*. What words can help you decide what kind of information to listen for?

_____

B 4.1 Listen and complete the *Exam Task*.

Exam Reminder

Understanding what to listen for
- Look for question words in the questions, for example, *When …?*, *How long …?* and *Where …?* to give yourself an idea of the type of information you need to listen for.
- Focus on what you need to listen for when you hear the recording.
- Remember that the questions are in the same order as the answers in the dialogue. You will hear the dialogue twice so you can check your answers.

Exam Task

Listen to Nia talking to her friend Sam about cooking. For each question, choose the right answer (**a**, **b** or **c**). You will hear the conversation twice.

1 Where are they going to cook?
  a Nia's house
  b Sam's house
  c a restaurant
2 What are they going to make?
  a sandwiches
  b a dessert
  c a big lunch
3 When are they meeting?
  a 1 pm
  b 2 pm
  c 3 pm
4 Why are they cooking the food?
  a Nia wants to practise.
  b Nia's family asked her to.
  c They're going to sell it.
5 How long does it take to cook in the oven?
  a 20 minutes
  b 35 minutes
  c about one hour

C 4.2 Listen again and check your answers.

4 A Day in the Life

Writing: an informal email

A Match the activities to the adjectives *boring*, *great*, *fun* and *exciting*. Use the adverbs *really* and *very* if you like.

1 clean the house   _____
2 go swimming   _____
3 see a play   _____
4 do exercise   _____
5 hang out in a café   _____
6 travel to another country _____

Learning Reminder

Using adjectives in emails
- Adjectives make your writing more interesting for the reader.
- Use positive and negative adjectives to describe your opinions better.
- For stronger opinions, use adverbs such as *really* and *very* before your adjectives.

B Read the writing task below and then circle the correct answer, a or b.

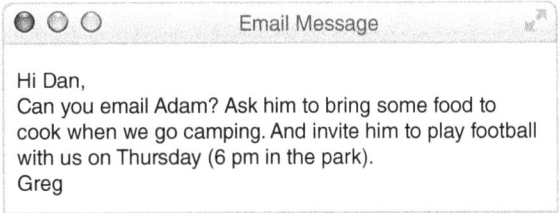

Hi Dan,
Can you email Adam? Ask him to bring some food to cook when we go camping. And invite him to play football with us on Thursday (6 pm in the park).
Greg

Read the email from your friend Greg about plans for next week. Write an email to Adam.
- *Tell him about the camping plans. Are you happy / unhappy about the plans?*
- *Then tell him about Thursday. Are you happy / unhappy about the plans?*
- *Find out if he can come on Thursday.*

Write 25–35 words.

1 a You are going to email Greg.
   b You are going to email Adam.
2 a You are going to write an informal email.
   b You are going to write a formal email.
3 a You are going to write about last week.
   b You are going to write about next week.

C Read the example email and complete it with these words.

excited   fun   great   looking   really

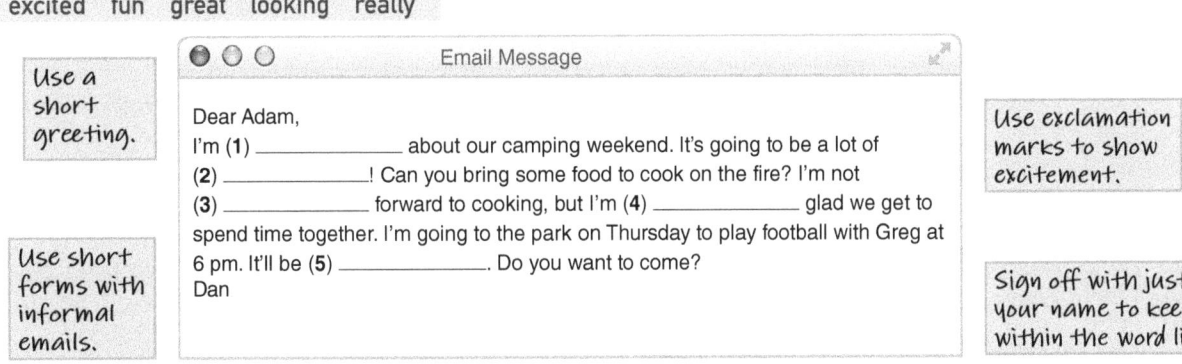

Use a short greeting.

Dear Adam,
I'm (1) _____ about our camping weekend. It's going to be a lot of (2) _____! Can you bring some food to cook on the fire? I'm not (3) _____ forward to cooking, but I'm (4) _____ glad we get to spend time together. I'm going to the park on Thursday to play football with Greg at 6 pm. It'll be (5) _____. Do you want to come?
Dan

Use exclamation marks to show excitement.

Use short forms with informal emails.

Sign off with just your name to keep within the word limit.

D Read and complete the *Exam Task* below. Don't forget to use the *Useful Expressions* on page 53 of your Student's Book.

Exam Task

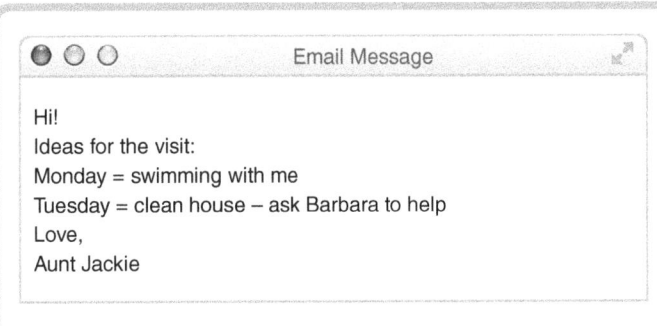

Hi!
Ideas for the visit:
Monday = swimming with me
Tuesday = clean house – ask Barbara to help
Love,
Aunt Jackie

Read the email from your aunt about plans to visit her. Write an email to Barbara.
- *Tell her about your plans for Monday. Are you looking forward / not looking forward to it?*
- *Then tell her about Tuesday. Are you looking forward / not looking forward to it?*
- *Find out if she can come.*

Write 25–35 words.

▶ Writing Reference p. 170 in Student's Book

Review 2

Vocabulary

A Choose the correct answers.

1 I can't believe it's 11 pm already. It's ___ late.
  a getting   c having
  b being   d doing
2 'Don't be late for your exam, Thomas.'
  'I know, Mum. I'll be there at 10 am ___.'
  a fast   c sharp
  b quick   d free
3 'Did you do anything last night?'
  'No, I stayed ___ and watched TV.'
  a over   c in
  b round   d out
4 When Jane came through the door, we threw ___ and said, 'Surprise!'
  a balloons   c candles
  b presents   d confetti
5 'Your brother's a really great guy.'
  'I know. I really look ___ to him.'
  a round   c forward
  b up   d in
6 How do you ___ with friends in other countries?
  a click   c contact
  b tick   d communicate
7 'You need to study for your maths exam.'
  'I know. I'm ___ time doing other things.'
  a using   c wasting
  b keeping   d spending
8 When Neil gets home from school, he ___ online straight away.
  a makes   c goes
  b takes   d does
9 Send the invitations by email. ___ mail takes forever.
  a Tail   c Snail
  b Sail   d Fail
10 A clock is a ___ that tells the time.
  a laptop   c computer
  b device   d desktop

11 'Let's go to the park, Jill.'
  'I can't. I have to ___ the carpet.'
  a sweep   c vacuum
  b iron   d dust
12 'Are you ready to leave?'
  'I need to ___ my hair, then we can go.'
  a brush   c take
  b make   d put
13 'Kyle, why didn't you ___ your bed this morning?'
  'Sorry, Mum. I forgot.'
  a make   c wash
  b do   d help
14 It's too windy to hang ___ the clothes to dry.
  a round   c up
  b from   d out
15 'What's the first thing you do in the morning?'
  'I always ___ a shower first.'
  a do   c make
  b get   d take
16 I sometimes ___ really tired after I go swimming.
  a do   c get
  b have   d be
17 'I can't believe I forgot my money.'
  'It's OK. You can ___ some from me.'
  a save   c borrow
  b make   d rent
18 I want to return these jeans, but I can't find the ___.
  a shelf   c receipt
  b till   d trolley
19 'Don't forget to stop at the baker's, Dan.'
  'Yes, I'll get a ___ of bread.'
  a jar   c packet
  b carton   d loaf
20 We usually get ___ late on Sunday mornings.
  a to   c at
  b up   d for

Grammar

B Choose the correct answers.

1 I ___ a train to Munich this afternoon.
   a take   c 'm taking
   b taking   d takes

2 Where ___ on holiday this summer?
   a you're going   c are you going
   b you go   d do you go

3 'What are your plans for Saturday?'
   'We ___ Ivan and Svetlana for lunch.'
   a 's meeting   c meet
   b meets   d 're meeting

4 ___ at the concert hall this week?
   a Is they playing   c Are they playing
   b Playing   d They are playing

5 'What happened to your skiing plans?'
   'I changed my mind. I ___.'
   a 'm going   c don't go
   b go   d 'm not going

6 Do you often eat dinner late ___ night?
   a on   c in
   b to   d at

7 'Where does Frank live?'
   'He lives ___ New York.'
   a for   c on
   b in   d at

8 They changed the exam day. It's ___ Tuesday now.
   a in   c at
   b of   d on

9 We're not going to Italy now. We're going ___ July.
   a on   c to
   b in   d at

10 Michael's dog got ___ a box and fell asleep.
   a from   c into
   b toward   d to

11 'Did you finally decide on a new coat?'
   'Yes, I ___ buy a red one.'
   a 'm going   c going to
   b 'm going to   d will

12 'It's really cold in here!'
   'OK. I ___ on the heating.'
   a 'm going to turn   c going to turn
   b 'll turn   d turn

13 I think I ___ for a walk now.
   a going to go   c 'll go
   b 'm going to go   d go

14 'Do you need music for the party?'
   'No, Steve ___ me with the music.'
   a 's going to help   c will help
   b going to help   d helps

15 I can't reach that glass. ___ get it for me, please?
   a Will you   c Are you going to
   b You   d You're going to

16 I need some ___ before I travel to Mexico.
   a bag   c information
   b passport   d ticket

17 There's only one ___ in the queue at the moment.
   a men   c women
   b people   d man

18 'Do you want milk in your coffee?'
   'No, but I'd like a ___ sugar in it, please.'
   a much   c few
   b little   d some

19 'How ___ food does a lion eat every day?'
   'Probably a lot!'
   a few   c many
   b some   d much

20 There are ___ of sheep in the countryside where I live.
   a many   c little
   b much   d lots

Review 2   Units 3 & 4   31

5 Home Sweet Home

Reading

A Read the *Exam Reminder*. Why is it important to be able to justify our answers?

_____

B Now complete the *Exam Task*.

> ### Exam Reminder
> **Justifying your answers**
> - We must be able to explain why we chose our answers.
> - If we can't justify our answer, it may be wrong. If this happens, try to explain the answer for another answer option. Do this with all of the answer options until you find the one that's correct.

Danica Hart

7th April – Old furniture … new!

I'm very excited today because I've finished cleaning and fixing my new bedroom furniture. Yes, as I've said in my other blog entries, it's not really 'new' furniture. I found it in the street! But with some love and care, it looks great! My dad helped me with some broken pieces. They were in really bad condition. But everything looks as good as new now and the headboard is beautiful. I love its simple design, like furniture from the countryside. You can see part of the headboard in my photo. I can't wait to chill out in my bedroom with all this cool 'old' furniture!

Jessica Albright

13th March – My helping hands

Today we started to build a new home. It's for a family that has a lot of money problems. They lost their home several years ago and life is very hard. I'm really amazed at how they stay together and keep strong. There are four family members, and the house we're building will have two bedrooms. I'm looking forward to finishing it. It will take us a couple of months to get everything ready, and then they can move in. I'm really glad I joined this organisation, Homes with Heart. I love building things, and working as a volunteer makes me love it even more!

Georgia Pataka

7th June – Putting the pieces back together

This week my family and I are travelling to Kefalonia, a Greek island on the west side of the country. We're going to visit my grandmother. She lives on the island, and she needs to find a new place to live for a while. There was an earthquake on the island, and it damaged her home. We're going to help her move to a new place. My grandmother can't live in her old house like it is. It's sad because my dad grew up in that house. It will take a very long time and a lot of money to fix it. Luckily, my grandmother has got some money saved up. But still, she'll have to live in a flat for a least a year. But on the bright side, I'm glad she'll have a nice place to live.

Exam Task

Read the blog entries of three teenagers. Choose the best answer (**a**, **b** or **c**) for each question.

1. Who is helping someone they've known for a very long time?
   a Danica
   b Jessica
   c Georgia
2. Who is working to make something useful again?
   a Danica
   b Jessica
   c Georgia
3. Who just started what they're doing?
   a Danica and Jessica
   b Danica and Georgia
   c Jessica and Georgia
4. Who is doing something with someone they're related to?
   a Danica and Jessica
   b Danica and Georgia
   c Jessica and Georgia
5. What is true about Danica's furniture?
   a It was free.
   b Someone gave it to her.
   c It's from the countryside.
6. What does Jessica say she loves doing?
   a working for free
   b building things
   c helping people move
7. What is good about Georgia's situation?
   a She's getting to visit her grandmother.
   b Her grandmother's home is easy to fix.
   c Her grandmother will have a lovely home.
8. Which blogger isn't doing something for someone else?
   a Danica
   b Jessica
   c Georgia

Vocabulary

A Complete the words in the sentences.

1. I'm excited about staying in my dad's holiday v _ _ _ _ over the summer.
2. They rented a very expensive f _ _ _ on the top floor of the building.
3. The doors to the kids' rooms are along this h _ _ _ _ _ _.
4. Her grandmother lives in a cute c _ _ _ _ _ _ 10 kilometres from town.
5. Can you put the milk in the f _ _ _ _ _ before it gets too warm?
6. We've only got one b _ _ _ _ _ _ _ _ in this house, so we have to wait if someone's taking a shower.

B Complete the dialogue with these words.

armchair   barbecue   cooker   lawnmower   tumble dryer   wardrobe

Mover: We're ready to move your furniture into the house. The first item is this (1) _____.
Donna: Yes, that goes in the utility room, which is at the back.
Mover: OK. And where would you like us to put this (2) _____?
Donna: I'd like you to put it in the living room, which is over there.
Mover: Great. And what about this (3) _____?
Donna: You can put that on the patio, behind the house. My husband loves cooking burgers outside.
Mover: And the (4) _____? I know it goes in the kitchen, but where is that?
Donna: It's at the back of the house as well.
Mover: OK. A couple more things … the (5) _____?
Donna: Yes, that goes in my bedroom. I'm looking forward to having something to put my clothes in finally. And the last thing?
Mover: The (6) _____.
Donna: Oh, yes. That goes in the shed, which is outside at the very back of the garden.

Home Sweet Home 5

C Circle the correct words.

1 This mirror / lamp is so dirty; I can't even see myself!
2 That's a really cool mat / poster on your wall!
3 Can you close the blinds / duvet? It's too sunny in here.
4 I don't like sleeping on this curtain / pillow because it is too hard.
5 Don't walk on the rug / mirror! Your shoes are not clean.
6 Sarah put an extra curtain / blanket on her bed because it was cold.
7 Can you get me my drink? I left it on the mat / coffee table.
8 Those are lovely curtains / paintings you've got on your windows.

D Complete the sentences with these words.

conditioner   dish   duvet   nomads   running   season   shelves   stove

1 My flat doesn't have _____ water at the moment, so I'm living with my brother.
2 The Apaches were originally _____, but most now live in homes.
3 My favourite _____ is summer because I like going to the beach when it's sunny.
4 Derek's cottage has a wood _____ in the living room so it is usually very warm, even in winter.
5 Can you put your books back on the _____ before you go out, please?
6 It's getting very warm. Will you switch on the air _____, please?
7 Dan's satellite _____ is broken, so he's coming here to watch the tennis match.
8 Do you prefer to have a blanket or a _____ on your bed?

E Read the *Exam Reminder* and complete the *Exam Task*.

Exam Task

Read Wolfgang's article about a special place in his garden. Write ONE word for each space.

My name's Wolfgang, and I live in the countryside in Germany. Behind our garden, I've (1) _____ a tree house, which is my special place. I love it there; I've got a small lamp with a battery. I can switch it (2) _____ and read a book. I've got a little wardrobe, so I can hang (3) _____ my jacket while I'm there. I've put (4) _____ some posters of animals and bands I like. I clean the tree house every week. I (5) _____ away all my things when I go back to my real home. Friends come to my tree house sometimes and they love chilling (6) _____ there!

Exam Reminder

Focusing on words before & after a gap

- Tasks that ask you to write only one word test your grammar and vocabulary skills.
- Look at the words before and after the gap. Do you see a grammatical structure, such as the Present Continuous, which might need *is* or *are*? Is it a set phrase or a phrasal verb, which needs a preposition or a verb?
- Think of words which often go together with the words around the gap. Try different words to see which one sounds best before you write your answer.

5 Home Sweet Home

Grammar

Present Perfect Simple; Possessives

A Complete the sentences with the Present Perfect Simple form of the verbs in brackets.

1 We _____ (go) to the bank already.
2 Dad _____ (clean) the whole kitchen.
3 I _____ (walked) 10 kilometres before.
4 She _____ (chose) to study history at university.
5 _____ (you buy) everything you need for the trip?
6 I _____ (never see) a pink elephant before.
7 He _____ (not eat) all of his breakfast yet!
8 _____ (you / not be) to Iceland before?

B Complete the sentences with *for* or *since*.

1 Mum has worked in a library _____ 1999.
2 She has studied at university _____ two years.
3 I haven't attended a concert _____ last March!
4 We have been in the sea _____ four hours.

C Circle the correct words.

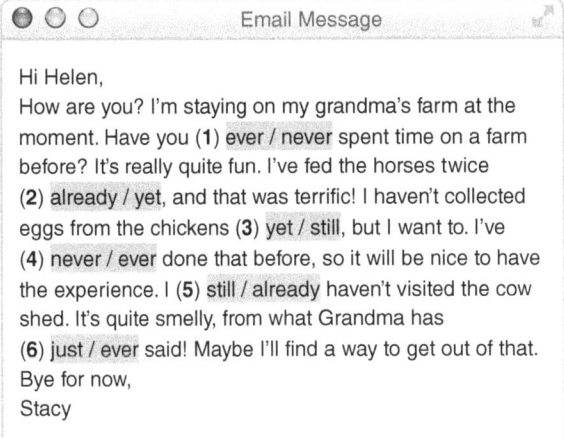

Hi Helen,
How are you? I'm staying on my grandma's farm at the moment. Have you (1) ever / never spent time on a farm before? It's really quite fun. I've fed the horses twice (2) already / yet, and that was terrific! I haven't collected eggs from the chickens (3) yet / still, but I want to. I've (4) never / ever done that before, so it will be nice to have the experience. I (5) still / already haven't visited the cow shed. It's quite smelly, from what Grandma has (6) just / ever said! Maybe I'll find a way to get out of that.
Bye for now,
Stacy

A group of chickens waiting for food

D Complete the sentences with the possessive form of the nouns in brackets.

1 Someone has just arrived at my _____ (neighbour) house.
2 _____ (James) dog has been in many fights.
3 These are the _____ (children) toys. They need to put them away!
4 Can you tell me where the _____ (ladies) toilet is, please?
5 I really need to clean my _____ (bird) cage!
6 That's not my book. That's _____ (Linda).

E Complete the dialogues with the correct possessive pronouns.

1 'Which car belongs to Glen and Becky?'
   '_____ car is the red one that's parked over there.'
2 'Is this your bag?'
   'No. _____ is the one that's on the shelf.'
3 'I can't find the room we're staying in.'
   'That's because _____ is on another floor.'
4 'I took the wrong coat by mistake.'
   'Yes, that is Rachel's coat. It belongs to _____.'

Home Sweet Home **5**

F Read the *Exam Reminder* and complete the *Exam Task*.

Exam Reminder

Identifying the kind of word you need
- When you look at the gaps in a text, think about the type of word that's missing.
- Look at all the words in your answer options carefully and think about what type of word they are. Often, there are only small differences between the words. You may have a set of possessive nouns, in which the singular and plural choices look almost the same.
- Check that your answer choice works in the sentence before you choose it as your answer.

Exam Task

Read the article about a type of home in Scandinavia. Choose the best word (**a**, **b** or **c**) for each space.

A home that moves with you

In northern Scandinavia, there is a group of people called the Sami. **(1)** ___ homes are known as lavvus, which look like tents. The difference is that **(2)** ___ are much stronger than the average tent, and they look much cooler, too! They **(3)** ___ lived in these types of homes **(4)** ___ hundreds of years. The lavvu works well for the lifestyle of a member of the Sami. It is a **(5)** ___ job to follow the deer that live in the area. So he needs a home that he can take with him.

The Sami build lavvus to protect them against strong winds. Traditionally, **(6)** ___ walls were deer skins, which did a good job of keeping out the cold. Nowadays, the Sami use different fabrics for the walls, which are like the kind we use for **(7)** ___ tents today. Of course, because of the cold, the Sami have to build fires inside the lavvu. But that's not a problem because **(8)** ___ got a hole at the top where smoke can escape.

1	a	Theirs	b	They	c	Their
2	a	their	b	his	c	theirs
3	a	have	b	has	c	are
4	a	by	b	since	c	for
5	a	his	b	Sami's	c	Sami
6	a	it	b	it's	c	its
7	a	ours	b	our	c	we
8	a	it's	b	its	c	it

A lavvu is a temporary dwelling used by the Sami people of northern Scandinavia.

Listening

A Read the *Exam Reminder*. What words in a dialogue tell us that an answer option may not be correct?

_____

B 🔊 5.1 Listen and complete the *Exam Task*.

Exam Reminder

Identifying the two incorrect options
- Remember to check you understand the question before you start.
- There is only one correct answer for each question, but the speakers will mention most of the answer options.
- Don't forget that the questions are in the same order as the answers.
- Listen for negative words or sentences connected with the answer options. This sometimes means it is not the correct answer and can help you identify the two incorrect answer options.

Exam Task

Listen to two friends talking about jobs around the house. Who does which job? For questions **1–5**, write a letter **A–G** next to each item. You will hear the conversation twice.

1. Julie ☐
2. Peter ☐
3. Sandra ☐
4. Hank ☐
5. Bill ☐

A clean the bathroom
B take care of the garden
C tidy the living room
D clean the bedroom
E tidy the patio
F do the washing up
G hang out the washing

C 🔊 5.2 Listen again and check your answers.

5 Home Sweet Home

Writing: a note

A Circle the correct words.

1. I didn't go to work today **because of** / **because** the weather.
2. There are too many people staying at our house. That's **because** / **why** you have to stay in a hotel.
3. I didn't call **because** / **because of** I didn't have my mobile with me.
4. This dinner just doesn't taste very nice. That's **why** / **because** Dad left it in the oven too long.

Learning Reminder

Explaining why

- We often give reasons in our writing to explain why we have done or haven't done things.
- Words and phrases like *because*, *because of*, *that's why* and *that's because* help us do this, and it's important to know what words follow them in order to use them properly.

B Read the schedule and the email and then decide if the statements are true (T) or false (F).

Sunday schedule

11 am	meet at Neil's house
12.30 pm	arrive at Corral River, have lunch
3.00 pm	go for hike round Mount Simmons
9.00 pm	come back home

Email Message

Hi Ryan,
Do you know what your plans are for the trip on Sunday yet? Let me know. Before you leave on Sunday, please take the dog for a walk. Also, will you be home for dinner at 7 pm? If so, I'd like you to go to the supermarket on the way home and get me some potatoes.
Have a great time!
Mum

1. Ryan's mum is going to Corral River on Sunday. ☐
2. Ryan is able to walk the dog on Sunday morning. ☐
3. Ryan is going to have dinner at home on Sunday. ☐

C Read the schedule and email in B again and correct the five mistakes in the example notes.

Make sure you transfer the correct information.

Don't get confused by similar numbers, dates, times, etc.

Hi Mum,
Just got your email about Sunday. We're meeting at Nile's house at 11 am, so I can take the cat out for a walk first. We're arriving at 1.30 and having lunch straight away. Then it's a hike to Mount Simons. I'm sorry, but I won't be home for dinner. That's why I'm not getting back until 9. Could Dad get the potatoes?
Ryan

Check your spelling.

Make sure you use the correct words to explain things.

D Read and complete the Exam Task below. Don't forget to use the Useful Expressions on page 67 of your Student's Book.

Exam Task

Read the email and the text message. Fill in the information in Andrea's note.

Email Message

Hi Andrea,
Give Skippy his food and post that letter to Aunt Leila. Also, I saw that they're having a sale at Brighton Books if you want to go there later. If not, send me an email and I'll stop and get that book you wanted. It's the book on Scottish castles, isn't it?
Love, Mum

From: Debbie
Guess what? I got an A on my exam! We're celebrating with pizza. It'll be here in half an hour. Come around at 1.30 if you can!

Mum, I gave (1) _____ something to eat and I went to the post office to send the letter to (2) _____. Thanks for letting me know about the book sale. I'm going to (3) _____ house later. She's having a celebration because she got an A on her exam. It starts at (4) _____, so that's why I'm not going to the book shop. The book I wanted is about (5) _____, like you said.
Hope you can get it for me!

Andrea

Home Sweet Home 5

6 The Place to Be

Reading

A Read the *Exam Reminder*. Do signs always use full sentences?

_____

B Now complete the *Exam Task*.

Exam Reminder

Using context to understand signs

- Signs and notices only use a few words, so it can be difficult to understand them. Think about where you would see each notice to help you work out the meaning.
- If you don't understand all of the words, look for words that you do understand to help you with the general meaning.
- Try to find words in the answer options that match what a sign or notice says.

Exam Task

Which sign (**A–H**) says this (**1–5**)?

1 You can't use your phone here. ☐
2 You cannot leave a car in this place. ☐
3 You need to be tall enough to do this. ☐
4 Animals cannot enter. ☐
5 If you have a problem, use this number. ☐

A Must be 130 cm to ride

B Do not feed the animals.

C For emergencies, call 0445100027.

D Please switch off mobiles while in hospital.

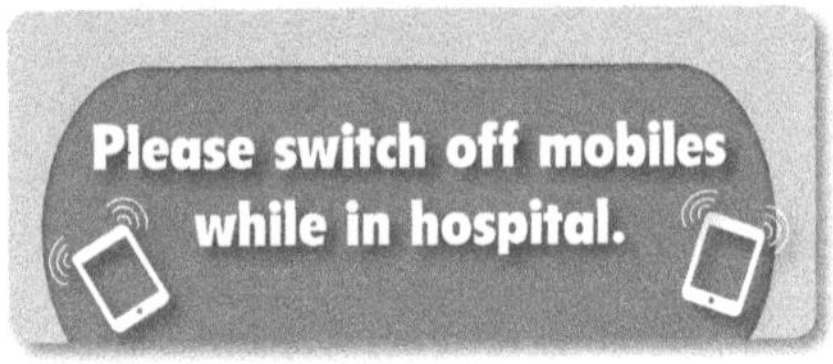

E No pets allowed

F Emergency phone

G NO PARKING allowed here

H Children under 12 must be with an adult.

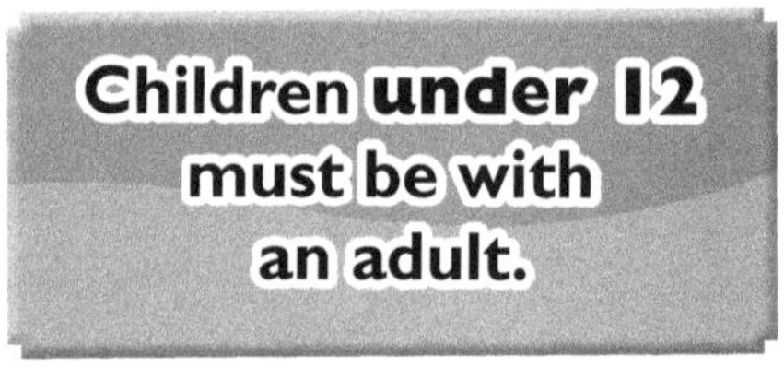

C Read the article. Which signs from B might you see in the place in the article?

One place, twice the fun!

There are many places to go to have fun. Stadiums, concerts, parks and theatres are some of these places. But what about going to two places in one? That's what Flamingo Land is. It's in North Yorkshire, England, and it was built in 1959. Originally, it was a large garden with lots of flamingos, which are large, pink birds with long legs. They usually live in tropical places like Florida. The gardens became popular, and after some years, the owners decided to build rides and bring different types of animals to live there. It's now both a zoo and an amusement park. So, if you like cool rides and want to see interesting animals, Flamingo Land is the place to be!

Vocabulary

A Complete the words for the places.

c _ _ _ _ _

t _ _ _ _ _ _

f _ _ _ _ _ _

p _ _ _ _ _ _ _

B Circle the correct words.

1 I can't make spaghetti because I've run into / out of pasta.
2 I don't feel well. I think I've come up / down with a cold.
3 My car hasn't got any petrol. I need to stop and fill up / in.
4 I need to take my laptop back to the shop because it broke off / down.
5 My sister is in a play that they're putting into / on at the local theatre.
6 I like being in the water, so I think I'll take over / up swimming.
7 James was late for the bus, so he ran through / along the street to the bus stop as fast as he could.
8 The traffic is very busy, so be careful when you walk across / under the street.
9 Have you seen Sarah's new hair cut? I walked through / past her in the street and I nearly didn't recognise her!
10 Can you get me that new computer game when you go into town? I don't want it to sell up / out before I get it.

C Look at the photo and tick the words that describe it.

1 boring ☐
2 crowded ☐
3 noisy ☐
4 peaceful ☐
5 polluted ☐
6 relaxing ☐

D Complete the text with these words.

bank   hospital   library   museum   post office   university

Jorge had a lot of things to do on Monday. First, he went to the (1) _____ to send a letter to a friend. Then he went to the (2) _____ to put some money in his account. After that, he attended two morning classes at (3) _____. During the afternoon break, he went to the (4) _____ to pick up a book. He also visited his aunt in (5) _____ to see if she was getting better. After his afternoon classes finished, he met Celia at the (6) _____ to see an exhibition. He was quite tired at the end of the day.

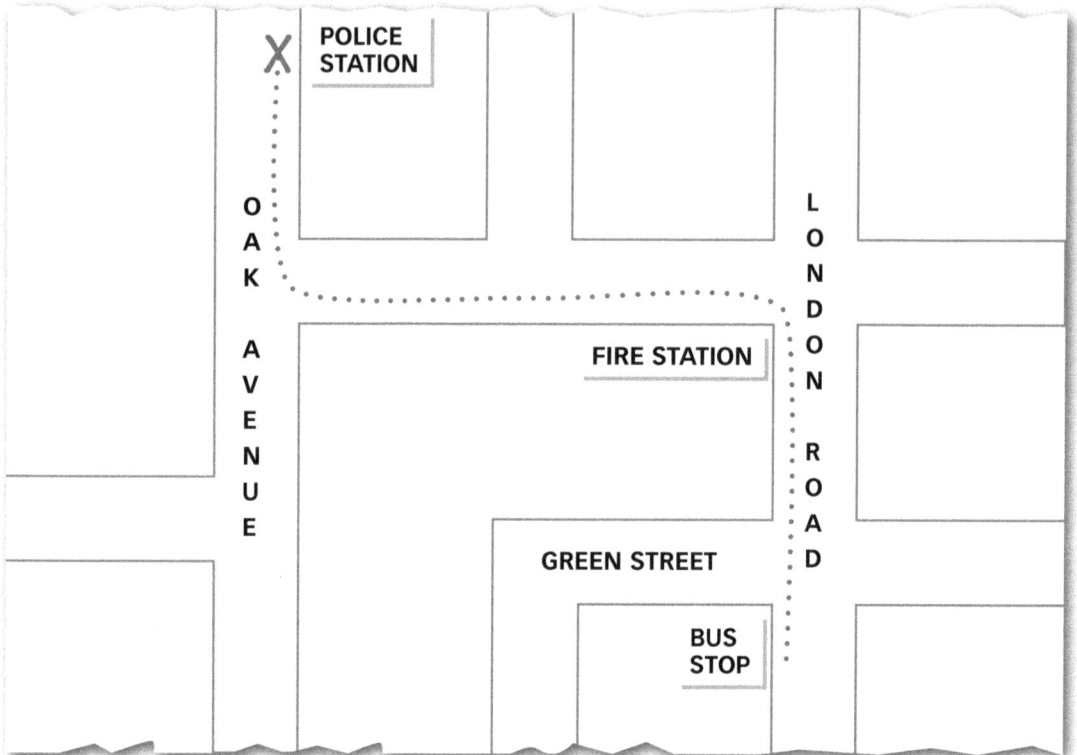

E Look at the map and circle the correct words to complete the directions.

1 You get on / off the bus at the bus stop on the corner of Green Street and London Road.
2 Then you cross / turn left at Green Street and go straight on until you get to the fire station.
3 Turn left / right at the fire station.
4 Next, follow the road until you get to / get on Oak Avenue.
5 Turn left / right at Oak Avenue.
6 Follow / Cross Oak Avenue to the police station and you're there!

6 The Place to Be

Grammar

Demonstratives; Articles

A Choose the correct answers.

1 Is there anyone sitting in ___ seat right here?
 a this   b these   c that
2 I'm not sure about ___ dresses over there. They're too bright.
 a this   b these   c those
3 ___ information is secret. Don't tell anyone!
 a This   b These   c Those
4 Do you know ___ woman? She's standing across the street.
 a this   b these   c that
5 ___ men in the café in the next street meet every Wednesday.
 a That   b Those   c These
6 Do you like ___ shoes? They make my feet look good, don't they?
 a this   b those   c these

B Complete the dialogue with *this*, *that*, *these* or *those*.

colonial farm house with a beautiful garden, South Africa

Gillian: I'm having a great time in South Africa, Mbeke. Thanks for showing me round your neighbourhood. (**1**) _____ place is really beautiful.

Mbeke: I'm glad you could come. See (**2**) _____ white house over there? That's my neighbour Daniel's house.

Gillian: Oh, right. The one with (**3**) _____ beautiful flowers in the garden. Are you friends?

Mbeke: Yes. Daniel's from the UK, like you. He helped me plant (**4**) _____ trees here in front of my house.

Gillian: They're really nice. He must know a lot about gardening.

Mbeke: He studied it at the University of Birmingham. Is (**5**) _____ university good?

Gillian: Yes, it is. It's one of the oldest universities in the UK. All of (**6**) _____ really old universities are quite good.

Mbeke: I hope to visit one of them some day!

C Complete the table with these words.

| Amazon | earth | Egypt | Himalayas | London | lunch | Mali | moon | Nile | Pacific | Paris | spaghetti |

the	no article

The Place to Be **6**

D Find and correct the mistakes in the sentences.

1 Every person needs the home, don't they? _____
2 I did a chores you asked me to do. _____
3 Is there an university in your town? _____
4 Tell Martin I'll be there in a hour. _____
5 How many countries are there in the Europe? _____
6 We're going skiing in an Alps this winter. _____
7 You can have a apple if you're hungry. _____
8 Have you ever been to the Texas? _____

E Complete the text with *a*, *an*, *the* or –.

We all need to go on (**1**) _____ adventure every now and again. This year, my family and I decided to sail across (**2**) _____ Atlantic Ocean. My parents have got (**3**) _____ really nice boat, so it was easy to make (**4**) _____ trip. Well, I say easy, but crossing (**5**) _____ ocean is hard work. It took us (**6**) _____ month to do it. We spent all our time on (**7**) _____ boat, and it was (**8**) _____ unique adventure, really. (**9**) _____ temperature was good, and there were no storms. It was also really nice to see (**10**) _____ moon at night, without (**11**) _____ single city light near us! I was sad when we reached (**12**) _____ Canada. I didn't want to go back on land!

Listening

A Read the *Exam Reminder*. Should you write phone numbers using words?
_____

B 6.1 ▶ Listen and complete the *Exam Task*.

Exam Task

You will hear some information about a sports centre. Listen and complete each question. You will hear the information twice.

Al's Sports Centre

Opening hours:	from 9.00 am to (**1**) _____ pm daily
Contact the manager:	telephone number (**2**) _____
Address:	(**3**) _____ Shelton Road
Monthly fee:	starts at (**4**) _____ pounds
Yoga class:	begins on (**5**) _____ September

Exam Reminder

Listening for days, times & numbers

- Remember to look at the gaps to work out what kind of information is missing. Sometimes this will be numbers, days or times.
- You can write the number as a figure (*7*), or you can write the word (*seven*). Remember to spell the number correctly. You can write times as either 7.15 or 7:15.
- When we say phone numbers, we say each number individually. For example, for *078*, we say 'oh seven eight' not 'oh seventy-eight'.

C 6.2 ▶ Listen again and check your answers.

6 The Place to Be

Writing: a formal email

A Put the directions in the correct order 1–4.

- ☐ Go up Charles Road until you get to Kings Street.
- ☐ The café, Coffee Grounds, is on your right.
- ☐ First, get off the bus at Charles Road.
- ☐ Then turn left at Kings Street and walk about 50 metres.

B Read the writing task below and then answer the questions.

Read the email from Amy Miller.

Email Message

To: Sherman Theatre

Dear Sir / Madam,
I have tickets for the play at Sherman Theatre next Saturday. I will be coming by bus. Is there a bus stop near the theatre? How can I get from the bus stop to the theatre? Also, can you tell me if there is food and drink available at the theatre?
I look forward to hearing from you.
Kind regards,
Amy Miller

Learning Reminder

Thinking about sequence

- Remember to put instructions explaining how to do something in the right order. This will make the instructions clear to the reader.
- Words like *first*, *next*, *then*, *before* and *after* show the order of each action.
- Remember to use the words with these structures when you give directions or other instructions: *before / after* + subject + verb (without *to*); *before / after* + noun; *before / after* + -ing; *first* + imperative; *first* + subject + verb; *then / next / after that* + imperative; *then / next / after that* + subject + verb; *eventually / finally* + subject + verb.

Write an email to Amy Miller and answer the questions. Write 40–60 words.

1 Do we know if Amy is writing to a man or a woman? _____
2 How many questions did Amy ask? _____
3 Should you write a formal or informal email? _____

C Read the example email and complete it with these words.

after dear get take then regards

Use a formal style of greeting.	**Email Message** To: Amy Miller (1) _____ Ms Miller, Thank you for your email. There is a bus stop near the theatre. (2) _____ the number 2 bus and (3) _____ off at Sydney Road. (4) _____ go down the street until you get to Richards Street. (5) _____ that, turn left and keep going for about 100 metres. The theatre is on the left. You can buy food and drink in the theatre café before or after the play. Best (6) _____, Jillian Fox Sherman Theatre Manager	*Remember to use a formal sign-off.*
Remember to answer all three questions in the email.		

D Read and complete the *Exam Task* below. Don't forget to use the *Useful Expressions* on page 79 of your Student's Book.

Exam Task

Read the email from Victor Wright.

Email Message

To: Bolton Stadium

Dear Sir / Madam,
I am writing to find out how to get to the stadium for the football match on Saturday. How can I get there from the city centre? I will be travelling by car. Is there a car park at the stadium? Also, can I bring snacks into the stadium?
I look forward to hearing from you.
Best regards,
Victor Wright

Write an email to Victor Wright and answer the questions. Write 40–60 words.

Review 3

Vocabulary

A Choose the correct answers.

1. My older sister lives in a ___ in a large building.
   - a hallway
   - b villa
   - c cottage
   - d flat

2. 'Where would you like me to put this coffee table?'
   'That goes in the ___.'
   - a living room
   - b dining room
   - c kitchen
   - d utility room

3. We have a ___ on our patio that we use in the summer.
   - a tumble dryer
   - b sofa
   - c barbecue
   - d cooker

4. 'Where do you keep your gardening equipment?'
   'It's in the ___ behind the house.'
   - a kitchen
   - b shed
   - c bedroom
   - d bathroom

5. This ___ is broken; I can't see my face clearly.
   - a painting
   - b duvet
   - c rug
   - d mirror

6. 'Larry, can you please put ___ your toys?'
   'Yes, Mum.'
   - a away
   - b off
   - c on
   - d in

7. We hung ___ our coats as soon as we arrived home.
   - a up
   - b in
   - c out
   - d round

8. I am really looking ___ to our holiday in Italy.
   - a for
   - b down
   - c forward
   - d up

9. Put your shoes on the ___ by the front door, please.
   - a duvet
   - b lamp
   - c mat
   - d curtain

10. 'I can't see.'
    'OK. I'll switch ___ a light.'
    - a back
    - b off
    - c up
    - d on

11. My favourite ___ is spring. I love all the flowers.
    - a garden
    - b factory
    - c season
    - d station

12. 'Why can't you make breakfast?'
    'Because we've run ___ eggs.'
    - a out of
    - b into
    - c over
    - d up

13. After class, Michelle went to the gym to work ___.
    - a round
    - b on
    - c over
    - d out

14. 'Did the customers like your cake?'
    'Yes, I sold ___ immediately.
    - a up
    - b out
    - c off
    - d on

15. His favourite football team was playing at the ___ near his house.
    - a disco
    - b corner shop
    - c stadium
    - d shopping centre

16. 'Why didn't you sleep well last night?'
    'The neighbours were playing music and it was so ___.'
    - a polluted
    - b relaxing
    - c peaceful
    - d noisy

17. 'The café is on the other side of the street.'
    'OK, let's ___ the street and go inside.'
    - a cross
    - b take
    - c turn
    - d follow

18. I saw a crime, so I went to the ___ to tell someone about it.
    - a fire station
    - b police station
    - c bank
    - d library

19. 'What did you do at the weekend?'
    'Not much. I just chilled ___ at home.'
    - a in
    - b onto
    - c at
    - d out

20. To get to my house, ___ bus number 5 to Oxford Street.
    - a do
    - b get
    - c take
    - d go

Grammar

B Choose the correct answers.

1 I don't want to see that film. I ___ it before.
   a was seeing   c saw
   b have seen   d see

2 They ___ a new sports centre across the street.
   a 've opened just   c 've just opened
   b opened just   d just have opened

3 We've lived here ___ 2010.
   a yet   c since
   b already   d for

4 ___ the washing up in the kitchen already?
   a Did you do   c Are you doing
   b You have done   d Have you done

5 'Why is Janie worried?'
   'She ___ by plane before.'
   a never travelled   c never has travelled
   b 's never travelled   d 's travelled

6 'Are you looking for something, sir?'
   'Yes, where is the ___ changing room?'
   a men   c mens'
   b mens   d men's

7 ___ notebook is the one with a picture of One Direction on it.
   a Jess   c Jesses
   b Jesss'   d Jess's

8 'I think I've picked up Fran's bag by mistake.'
   'Yes, that looks like ___.'
   a she   c her
   b yours   d hers

9 'Which one of these houses belongs to Mark and Dana?'
   '___ house has the red door.'
   a His   c Theirs
   b Her   d Their

10 'This is my video game, Bobby.'
   'No, it's ___. Mum said we had to share it.'
   a mine   c ours
   b theirs   d his

11 'Do you like the jeans here in front of you?'
   'No, I like ___ jeans on the shelf over there.'
   a those   c these
   b this   d that

12 ___ TV programme is awful. I'm changing the channel.
   a These   c This
   b Those   d That

13 'Excuse me, driver. Does ___ bus take you to the city centre?'
   'No, you need to take that bus over there.'
   a that   c these
   b those   d this

14 'The team's new uniforms look great.'
   'Yes, but I don't like ___ shoes they're wearing.'
   a those   c that
   b these   d this

15 Yolanda is from ___ Nigeria.
   a a   c –
   b an   d the

16 Have you ever sailed down ___ river Nile?
   a an   c a
   b the   d –

17 I like Gillian because she's ___ honest person.
   a –   c an
   b the   d a

18 'A flat needs a fridge, a cooker and a washing machine.'
   'Yes, but ___ flat I stayed in had none!'
   a a   c –
   b an   d the

19 I would rather live in ___ ugly house than no house at all.
   a –   c an
   b a   d the

20 We visited ___ Rocky Mountains last year and went skiing.
   a an   c the
   b a   d –

7 Time Out!

Reading

A Read the *Exam Reminder*. What can replace nouns in the answer options?

_____

B Now complete the *Exam Task*.

Exam Reminder
Looking for connections (pronouns)
- Quickly read the conversations to get a basic idea of the meaning.
- Pay attention to the pronouns or nouns in the conversations (e.g. *homework*). Then look for nouns or pronouns that match them in the answer options (e.g. *it*). This can help you eliminate wrong answers as well.

Exam Task

Part 1

Complete the five conversations.
Choose the answer **a**, **b** or **c**.

1. Does Mary know how to walk a tightrope?
   a Yes, I do.
   b She's over there.
   c Yes, she does.
2. Have you done your homework for the science class yet?
   a We're studying robots.
   b I'm doing it later tonight.
   c Of course, let's do it now.
3. I've ridden a unicycle before.
   a Yes, I have.
   b Is it difficult to ride?
   c Haven't you?
4. How about going to the circus at the weekend?
   a That's a great idea.
   b You can go if you like.
   c I'm busy on Thursday.
5. Why didn't you come to the book club?
   a I didn't have time to read it.
   b I was busy studying for exams.
   c You've never been before.

Part 2

Complete the conversation between two friends.
What does Paula say to Kelly? Choose from **A–H**.

Kelly: Have you practised a lot for the theatre performance this Saturday, Paula?
Paula: (6) ____
Kelly: Great! You must be ready for the big night, then.
Paula: (7) ____
Kelly: I'm sure you'll be fine. I'll be there for support!
Paula: (8) ____
Kelly: What time does the show start and how long does it last?
Paula: (9) ____
Kelly: Great. Well, I'm looking forward to seeing it. I'm bringing my little sister with me as well. She's very excited, too.
Paula: (10) ____
Kelly: Of course! Well, I'll see you on the opening night!

A Thanks, I appreciate that!
B It's at the Oakville Theatre on Harris Street.
C Yes, I have. For hours and hours, actually.
D Of course she can come. I'd love to meet her.
E At 7 pm sharp and the play is two hours long.
F Oh, great! I'd like to meet her after the show.
G No, thanks. I'll be just fine.
H I am, but I don't know if I have much confidence.

An actress performing in a Chinese musical

C Read the article. Which conversations from B, Part 1 relate to the place in the article?

Have fun AND make money!

Can your love of entertainment make you rich? That's what happened to one man, Guy Laliberté. He began his career as a street performer in Montreal in the 1970s. He used to play the accordion and he was also a fire eater! He was a big fan of the circus, and in 1984, he and a friend started a company, known as Cirque du Soleil, that puts on circus performances. The performers do a variety of acts and dance shows that wow audiences. His shows became very successful, and today Laliberté is one of the richest people in the world. That's very impressive for someone who used to play music and eat fire in the streets!

Vocabulary

A Where would you use these items or do these hobbies? Complete the table with these words. Some words may go in both columns.

brushes   camera   camping   controller   gaming   guitar   photography   sleeping bag   tent   video game

Outside	Inside

B Circle the correct words.
1 Mark doesn't like sleeping in a tent / guitar because he likes to look at the sky at night.
2 He played his new video game / controller for four hours yesterday.
3 What kind of camera do you use for your music / photography class?
4 When did you first learn how to play the sleeping bag / guitar?
5 This type of brush / stick is good for painting landscapes.
6 Darla used a lot of red and green camera / paint in her art project.

C Circle the correct words.
1 I'd like to go to a song writing class. Are you interested at / to / in joining me?
2 I'm not very keen to / at / on that band, so I don't listen to their music.
3 Everybody's crazy about / in / for that actor, but I don't like his films.
4 If you tell me what you're searching to / for / at, I can help you find it.
5 Paul's really for / into / in skateboarding at the moment. Let's buy him a new skateboard for his birthday.
6 Have you done / had / been your hobbies for a long time?

Time Out! **7**

D Complete the text with these words.

active boring creative exciting relaxing unusual

My sister Carrie and I are two completely different people when it comes to hobbies. Carrie likes being very (1) _____ and playing sports like basketball and football. She thinks it's (2) _____ to get together with friends on a team and exercise while having fun. For me, though, I prefer doing something (3) _____ like drawing or making music. It's quite (4) _____ to make something beautiful or interesting. But Carrie thinks what I do is very (5) _____. She doesn't find art interesting at all. Is it (6) _____ for two sisters to be so different? Or are there many other siblings who are just as different from each other as we are?

E Complete the sentences with these words.

athletics chess hiking sailing table tennis yoga

1 You lose a game of _____ when the other player takes your king.
2 Can you still go _____ in your boat if the weather's bad?
3 I'm more relaxed now because I do a(n) _____ class.
4 We do many different types of _____ at school, such as running, jumping and throwing.
5 I'm not good at _____ because I can't hit the ball properly!
6 I've never gone _____ up that mountain, but I think it would be fun.

F Read the *Exam Reminder* and complete the *Exam Task*.

Exam Reminder

Using prepositions
- A lot of multiple-choice tasks ask you to complete texts with prepositions, such as *in*, *for* and *about*.
- The texts often have set phrases and collocations in which the preposition is part of the phrase. Look at the words surrounding the gaps and see if you can work out which preposition might fit.

Exam Task

Read the article about toy collecting.
Choose the best word (**a**, **b** or **c**) for each space.

A kid at heart

Stan may be 32 years old, but he feels 12! He is very involved (1) ___ toy collecting, and he has collected thousands of toys over the years. He simply (2) ___ stop collecting them, but that's because he loves toys so much. He's a big fan (3) ___ toy cars and he owns over 3,000 different types. He spends quite a lot of time (4) ___ his hobby every week. It's not all about playing, though. He writes reviews of toys and he shares them with other people on the internet. His wife sometimes laughs about his hobby. '(5) ___ about getting a real hobby?' she says as a joke. 'Why don't you learn to (6) ___ chess or go hiking instead?' His two daughters, on the other hand, love that their dad plays with toys (7) ___ his free time. The three of them have a great time together (8) ___ the weekend, and sometimes their mum even joins in, too!

1 a for   b in   c on
2 a can't   b don't   c can
3 a over   b of   c for
4 a on   b in   c to
5 a Why   b Which   c How
6 a play   b do   c go
7 a on   b to   c in
8 a this   b in   c at

48 **7** Time Out!

Grammar

Conditionals: Zero & First; Gerunds; Infinitives

A Write zero conditional sentences with these words.

1 when / Stan / finish / his homework early / he / play / video games
___
2 if / I / not have / money / I / stay at home
___
3 when / it / snow / we / not go / outside
___
4 I / always lose / when / I / play chess / with Dan
___
5 Kyle / wake up / late / if / his alarm / not go / off
___
6 you / win / free tickets / if / you / guess / the right answer
___
7 when / the bus / be / late / I / walk / to school
___
8 water / freeze / if / the temperature / be / 0°C
___

B Complete the sentences with the first conditional form of the verbs in brackets.

1 If you buy the puzzle, I _____ (**help**) you do it.
2 If Grandma _____ (**come**) for a visit this weekend, we will play cards.
3 I _____ (**buy**) a new toy dinosaur if Mum gives me the money for it.
4 If they _____ (**not get**) here soon, we'll leave without them.
5 Gerard will save us a seat at the theatre if we _____ (**ask**) him to.
6 If they don't clean this pool, I _____ (**not swim**) here again.
7 I _____ (**cook**) some pizza if you are hungry later.
8 If Sarah _____ (**not do**) her homework properly this time, Dad will be really annoyed.

C Complete the sentences with the gerund or infinitive form of the verbs in brackets.

1 _____ (**paint**) is one of my favourite things to do.
2 We can't go _____ (**sail**) this weekend because it's going to be too windy.
3 My sister is old enough _____ (**join**) a gymnastics club.
4 Tom left _____ (**meet**) his friends at the skate park.
5 I'm not too keen on _____ (**read**), as I prefer films.
6 I was sad _____ (**hear**) that Jake's team lost the match.
7 John's looking forward to _____ (**start**) the photography lessons next week.
8 It's silly _____ (**worry**) about the test. You'll definitely pass!

Time Out! **7**

D Read the *Exam Reminder* and complete the *Exam Task*.

Exam Reminder

Looking at the whole text
- Before you try to answer the questions, read through the whole text first to get a basic understanding of it.
- When you write conditional sentences, remember to use the correct verb forms. For other structures, think about whether you need a gerund or infinitive form after a verb.
- Remember that for some of the gaps, you might need a negative word, such as *not* or *never*. Read the whole sentence to see if a negative word fits best in the gap.

Exam Task

Complete the blog about a concert. Write ONE word for each space.

The early bird gets a front-row seat

(1) _____ you want (2) _____ see your favourite performer for free, you had (3) _____ get up early to queue. It's especially hard to do this if you hate (4) _____ out of bed at 4 am like me! But that's exactly what I (5) _____. It was a free One Direction concert, so of course I couldn't miss it. I left my house at 4.30 am, and I was too tired (6) _____ walk. I met my friends at Rigley Stadium at 5 am and I was (7) _____ happy to see 100 people already in the queue. My friends saw how tired I was, and they asked if I (8) _____ rather leave and go back to bed, but I decided to stay. In the end, we stood – and sometimes sat – in the queue (9) _____ sixteen hours. Can you believe that? But, we got a space (10) _____ the front of the stage and the concert was great!

Listening

A Read the *Exam Reminder*. What does a phrase like *in fact* tell us about the speaker's opinion of what the other speaker has said?

_____

B 🔊 7.1 Listen and complete the *Exam Task*.

Exam Reminder

Listening for clues
- Exam task conversations sometimes involve people talking about whether something is true or not.
- Words like *absolutely*, *you're right*, etc. tell us that the speaker agrees with the other speaker, or thinks something is true, and words like *actually*, *in fact* and *but* tell us that someone is probably going to disagree with the other speaker and correct him or her.
- It's important to listen carefully when speakers correct each other because it will help you decide on the correct answers.

Exam Task

Listen to Sylvia and Patrick talking about their friends and different activities. What does each person do in their free time? For questions **1–5**, write a letter **A–G** next to each person. You will hear the conversation twice.

1. Patrick ☐
2. Sylvia ☐
3. Louis ☐
4. Miranda ☐
5. Hamish ☐

A reading magazines
B playing video games
C talking on the phone
D chatting online
E going hiking
F swimming
G gardening

C 🔊 7.2 Listen again and check your answers.

50 **7** Time Out!

Writing: an advert

A Complete the suggestions with the correct form of the verbs in brackets.

1. Would you like _____ (see) a play this weekend?
2. How about _____ (call) Jo to see if he can come?
3. Maybe we could _____ (bring) your sister with us.
4. What about _____ (go) out after the film finishes?

B Read the email and the notes and then decide if the sentences are true (T) or false (F).

> **Email Message**
>
> Hi Tina,
> The juggling competition is on Sunday and you said you want to help. I know you are creative, so would you be interested in making the advert? What about coming to my house tomorrow to discuss design ideas? Please say yes because you're so good at art!
> Bye for now,
> Martin

> JUGGLING COMPETITION
> 2 pm
> At Wilkinson Park
> Sandwiches (£2.50) and drinks (£1) on sale
> Costs £5

Learning Reminder

Making suggestions & persuading
- We can make suggestions in different ways.
- Sometimes we use the infinitive form with a structure such as *Would you like* **to go** *swimming*? Sometimes we use a noun or a gerund, such as *How about* **watching** *a film*? Sometimes we use a pronoun and the infinitive without *to*, such as *Maybe we could* **try** *the new restaurant*.
- When we want to persuade people to do something, we often use an imperative and a reason, such as ***Eat*** *your vegetables.* ***They're good for you***. We use *do not* or *don't* before the imperative to make it negative.

1. Martin wants Tina to enter the juggling competition. ☐
2. The competition is at Martin's house. ☐
3. You need to bring your own snacks to the competition. ☐

C Read the email and notes in B again and underline the incorrect information on the example advert.

> Remember that both texts have important information.

Are you bored just watching TV? Then why don't you come to
MEMFORD'S JUGGLING COMPETITION?
The competition is at 3 pm on Sunday at Wilkins Park.
Admission: £10
Pizzas are on sale for £2.50 and drinks are £1.50.
Join us – you won't regret it!

> Remember to use the important information from the two texts to help you complete the text.

D Read and complete the *Exam Task* below. Don't forget to use the *Useful Expressions* on page 93 of your Student's Book.

Exam Task

Read Tom's notes and Charlotte's email. Fill in the information on Tom's advert.

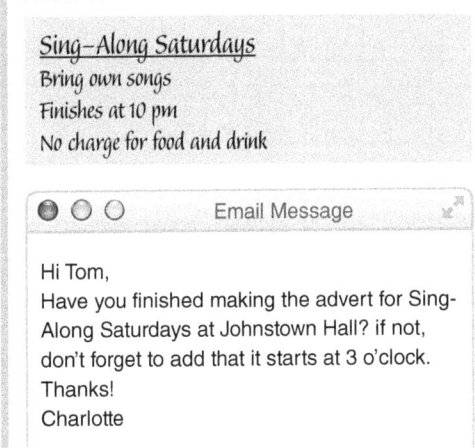

Sing-Along Saturdays
Bring own songs
Finishes at 10 pm
No charge for food and drink

Email Message

Hi Tom,
Have you finished making the advert for Sing-Along Saturdays at Johnstown Hall? if not, don't forget to add that it starts at 3 o'clock.
Thanks!
Charlotte

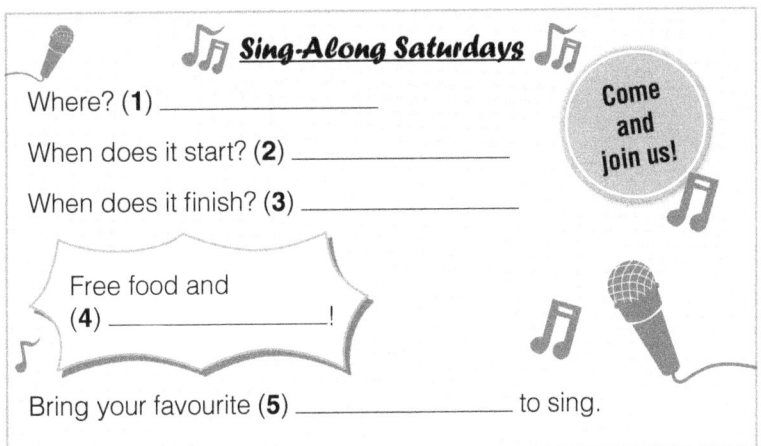

🎵 *Sing-Along Saturdays* 🎵

Where? (1) _____

When does it start? (2) _____

When does it finish? (3) _____

Free food and
(4) _____!

Bring your favourite (5) _____ to sing.

Come and join us!

▶ Writing Reference p. 172 in Student's Book

8 Personal Best

Reading

A Read the *Exam Reminder*. What are synonyms?
_____

B Now complete the *Exam Task*.

Exam Reminder

Looking for words with similar meanings
- You will see words in the signs and notices that have similar meanings to words in the sentences, such as *safe / secure* and *help / assistance*.
- Find these synonyms and underline them to help you do the matching task correctly.

Exam Task

Which notice (**A–H**) says this (**1–5**)?

1. You can get balls, bats and gloves at a discount.
2. Don't leave empty drinks bottles here.
3. You should write your name down to join these classes.
4. The sea is dirty, so you can't go in the water.
5. If you discover any missing things, please take them to reception.

A Sign up for yoga and aerobics here. First lesson is free. Call Sandy for more information on 0448943882.

B Special offer on sports equipment. This weekend only at Sam's Sports Shop.

C Please bring any lost items that you find to the front desk. Thank you.

D Ticket office at the main entrance of the stadium on Broad Street.

E Keep personal items with you at all times.

F For your own safety, do not run next to the pool.

G WARNING – beach area unsafe for swimming due to pollution.

H Help keep our stadium clean – take your rubbish with you when you leave.

Emirates Stadium is the home of Arsenal Football Club

C Read the article. Which notices from B might you see where the athletes do their training?

Getting the Olympic Gold

What do you need to do to become an Olympian? You might think you need to do hours of training, eat healthy food and do a lot of exercise, and you are right! But it also depends on what type of athlete you want to be.

Take swimmers, for example. They have to learn how to move their arms, legs and body in water. If you want to be a fast swimmer, known as a sprinter, you only spend a couple of hours in the pool every day. It's all about speed, so you work on your moves and how you do them. If you want to become a distance swimmer, then how long you can swim for is the most important thing to work on. Distance swimmers can swim up to 15 kilometres at a time when they train. That's about six hours in the pool for every day of practice. So whatever sport you want to do, to become an Olympian you've got to REALLY love it!

Vocabulary

A Complete the sentences with these words.

ball   bat   court   goal   pitch   racket

1 The cricket players got together on the _____ to get ready for the match.
2 We play basketball at a _____ in the gym near my house.
3 When you play cricket, be careful not to hit anyone with your _____!
4 The football player scored the winning _____ with two seconds left in the match.
5 Because she didn't get the _____ over the net, she lost the match.
6 I can't play tennis today because I need to buy a new _____.

B Read the questions and complete the words.

1 Who makes the players follow the rules?
   r _ _ _ _ _ _
2 Who is the person you play against in a sport?
   o _ _ _ _ _ _ _
3 What type of athlete jumps into water from a high board?
   d _ _ _ _
4 What do you call a person who loves a team very much?
   f _ _
5 Who's the person that looks after a sports team or player?
   m _ _ _ _ _ _
6 Which sports person rides a bike?
   c _ _ _ _ _ _
7 What do you call the football player who catches the ball?
   g _ _ _ _ _ _ _ _
8 Who is the person that travels in a boat?
   s _ _ _ _ _

C **Complete the table with these words.**

athletics   cycling   diving   gymnastics   sailing   swimming

do	go

D **Complete the sentences with the correct form of these words.**

beat   coach   lose   race   score   serve   take part   win

1 Stefan was very happy that his team _____ the match.
2 Helena kicked the ball and _____ a goal.
3 Next weekend I'm going to _____ in an athletics competition.
4 Meredith was nervous because it was her turn to _____ the ball to the other team.
5 Michael's dad _____ a team of 12-year-old basketball players at weekends.
6 Let's _____ to the end of the street to see who can run fastest.
7 The Sentinels _____ the Kicks by 74-58 in the basketball tournament.
8 I promise I won't drop out of the team if we _____ this game.

E **Complete the dialogue with one word in each gap.**

Sandra: Hey, Barry. How's your swimming practice going?
Barry: Oh, it's really terrible. Sometimes I feel like (**1**) _____ up!
Sandra: Oh, no. I hope you're not going to (**2**) _____ out of the swimming class.
Barry: No, it's just very difficult and it's so tiring, too. After just ten minutes, it's hard to (**3**) _____ going and some races can go (**4**) _____ for twenty minutes! At the end of the practice, I feel like I'm going to (**5**) _____ out.
Sandra: That's frustrating. Do you warm (**6**) _____ before you swim by jogging or stretching?
Barry: Yes. I also (**7**) _____ out at the gym three times a week, so I'm quite fit already.
Sandra: Hmm. So how long have you been swimming?
Barry: This is my first week. I thought I would like it, but now I'm not sure.
Sandra: Well, try to (**8**) _____ strong and keep doing it. Maybe it will get better over time. It's only been a week.
Barry: Maybe you're right. Thanks for your advice!
Sandra: Good luck!

54 **8 Personal Best**

Grammar

Modals (1); Modals (2)

A Circle the correct words.

1. A: Is it OK to run in the classroom?
   B: No, you should / can't.
2. A: I have so much work to do at home.
   B: Shall / Should I help you do some of it?
3. A: I'm sorry you didn't win the match.
   B: That's OK because I shall / can't win the next one!
4. A: May / Should we play football in your front garden?
   B: Of course. That's fine.
5. A: Your dad looks very fit.
   B: When he was young, he could / can run a kilometre in four minutes.
6. A: Have you got any advice for playing volleyball well?
   B: You should / may practise every day.
7. A: Oh, no! I've lost my tennis racket.
   B: Don't worry. You could / can borrow mine.
8. A: If you want to be a professional athlete, you can / can't miss too many practice sessions.
   B: I know. I'm too lazy!

B Write sentences with these words and the correct modal for the prompts in brackets.

1. they / practise / cricket daily (*give advice*)
   _____
2. I / win / the competition on Saturday (*express a strong intention*)
   _____
3. Mikey / swim / when he was four (*say what someone was able to do*)
   _____
4. I / join / the volleyball team (*ask for advice*)
   _____
5. you / go in / the pool today (*refuse permission*)
   _____
6. I / carry / the racket for you (*offer to do something*)
   _____

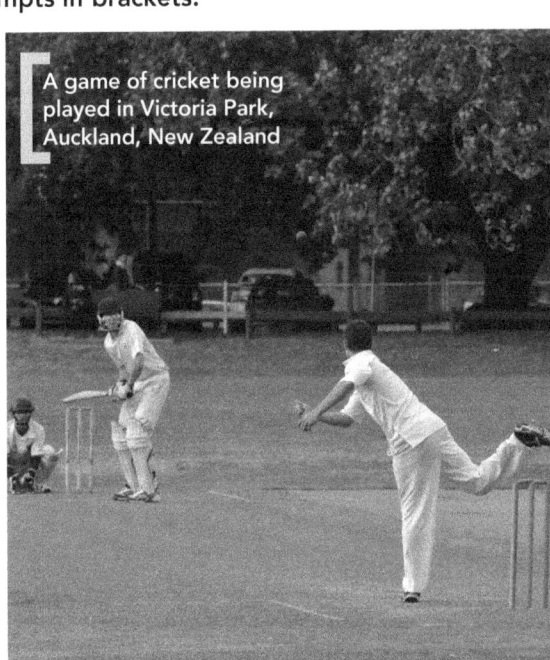

A game of cricket being played in Victoria Park, Auckland, New Zealand

C Complete the sentences with these words.

don't have   have   have   must   must   mustn't   needn't

1. The last day to sign up for the marathon is Saturday, so you _____ do it before then.
2. I'm bringing water to the event, so you _____ to.
3. You _____ to be at least ten years old to do this sport.
4. We _____ be late for the match, or we'll get really bad seats.
5. It will be cloudy today, so you _____ wear your sunglasses.
6. Sarah _____ wear proper boots when we go hiking.
7. Do I _____ to go to the basketball game? I hate basketball!

Personal Best **8**

D Circle the correct words to complete the monologue.

Welcome to Sammy's Riding Club. First, I'd like to discuss a few rules. Before you get on the horse, you (**1**) must / have check the saddle, which is the seat, is on correctly, but you (**2**) don't have / needn't worry about doing it alone. Someone will help you with it. Of course, you (**3**) don't have to / must buy your own boots and helmet because we've got everything here. You (**4**) mustn't / have to stay on the horse riding paths. You (**5**) needn't / mustn't leave the paths because you or the horse could get hurt. Also, you (**6**) don't have to / mustn't give the horses any food. They have a special diet so they stay healthy and strong. We'll ride for one hour today, so we (**7**) needn't / must return to the centre by 4 pm. I'll let you know when it's time to go back, so you (**8**) have to / don't have to look at your watch all the time! OK, let's get ready to ride!

[A young girl going out for a ride on her horse in the countryside]

Listening

A Read the *Exam Reminder*. Should you use *seven* or *seventh* when you say the date *7th June*?

_____

B 8.1 ▶ Listen and complete the *Exam Task*.

Exam Task

You will hear a woman on the radio talking about a rock climbing class. Listen and complete each question. You will hear the information twice.

Rock climbing near you

Join from the (**1**) _____ of the month.

The class can have up to (**2**) _____ climbers.

You must be at least (**3**) _____ years of age to join.

Fee: (**4**) _____ pounds for a five-week course

For more information, call the gym on (**5**) _____.

Exam Reminder

Listening for numbers & dates
- Some numbers sound similar, so listen carefully for what number the speaker is actually saying.
- Think about whether the number makes sense in the context. For example, some dates (such as *60th February*) could not be correct.
- When you say a date, remember to use *first, second, third, fourth*, etc. instead of *one, two, three, four*.

C 8.2 ▶ Listen again and check your answers.

8 Personal Best

Writing: a blog

Learning Reminder

Using the correct tense
- Remember to use the right tense to write about events that happened in the past.
- We use the past simple for actions that happened one after the other, or for actions that happened at one time in the past. We use the past continuous if we want to talk about an event that happened for a longer period of time in the past.

A Write sentences with these words and past tenses.

1 Tom / play / football / when / he / get / hurt
   _____

2 yesterday / I / go / swimming / and / run / in a race
   _____

3 I / look forward / meet the cricket legend
   _____

4 we / win / but then / the other team / score
   _____

B Read the writing task below and then circle the correct words.

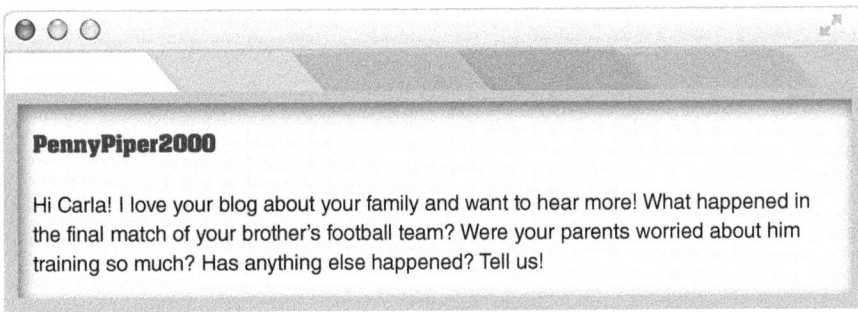

PennyPiper2000

Hi Carla! I love your blog about your family and want to hear more! What happened in the final match of your brother's football team? Were your parents worried about him training so much? Has anything else happened? Tell us!

Read the comment on a blog.
Write a blog post and answer the questions. Write 35–45 words.

1 PennyPiper2000 writes / doesn't write a blog.
2 You have to write a description of an event / a person.
3 You have to / don't have to answer all three questions.

C Read the example blog and complete it with these words.

badly   disaster   great   hard   upset   well

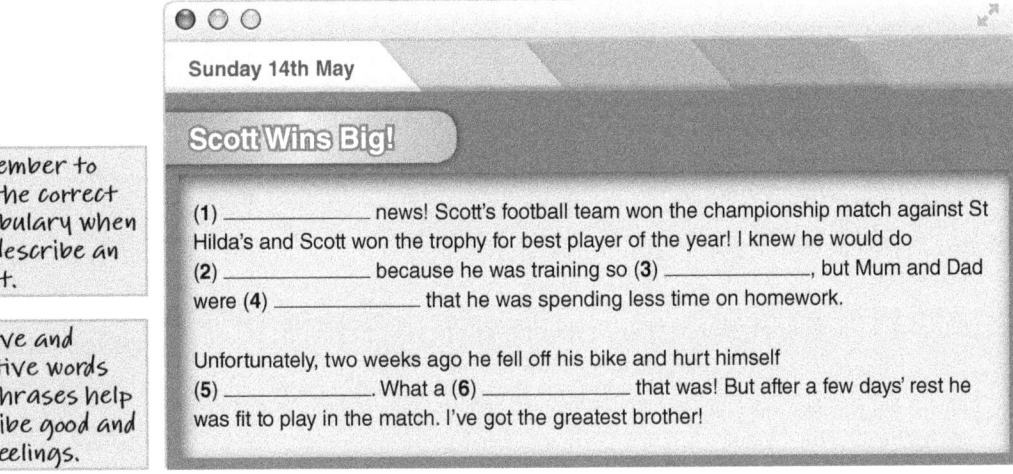

Sunday 14th May

Scott Wins Big!

(1) _____ news! Scott's football team won the championship match against St Hilda's and Scott won the trophy for best player of the year! I knew he would do (2) _____ because he was training so (3) _____, but Mum and Dad were (4) _____ that he was spending less time on homework.

Unfortunately, two weeks ago he fell off his bike and hurt himself (5) _____. What a (6) _____ that was! But after a few days' rest he was fit to play in the match. I've got the greatest brother!

Remember to use the correct vocabulary when you describe an event.

Positive and negative words and phrases help describe good and bad feelings.

Make your description interesting with adjectives and adverbs.

D Read and complete the *Exam Task* below. Don't forget to use the *Useful Expressions* on page 105 of your Student's Book.

Exam Task

Read the email from your friend, Jessie.

Email Message

Did you enjoy your first day at volleyball practice? How long did you play for? Did anything exciting happen? Tell us about it in your blog.
Jessie

Write a blog post and answer the questions. Write 35–45 words.

Review 4

Vocabulary

A Choose the correct answers.

1. I enjoy ___ because I like using a camera.
   - a gaming
   - b music
   - c photography
   - d camping

2. I need a new ___ for my painting class.
   - a brush
   - b tent
   - c guitar
   - d controller

3. Jill loves sport because she likes being ___.
   - a unusual
   - b boring
   - c creative
   - d active

4. 'What are you going to bring on the camping trip?' 'I'll definitely take my ___.'
   - a instrument
   - b video game
   - c paint
   - d sleeping bag

5. We're going ___ this weekend, so remember to take good boots.
   - a shopping
   - b swimming
   - c sailing
   - d hiking

6. I'm not good at playing ___. I lose every time.
   - a chess
   - b yoga
   - c gymnastics
   - d athletics

7. 'What do you do ___ your free time, Sara?' 'I paint or read books.'
   - a to
   - b at
   - c in
   - d on

8. My grandma ___ a lot of hobbies.
   - a is
   - b has
   - c goes
   - d takes

9. 'How ___ seeing a play on Sunday?' 'Sounds great!'
   - a for
   - b to
   - c about
   - d with

10. ___ is great fun if you play on the beach.
    - a Ice hockey
    - b Basketball
    - c Volleyball
    - d Tennis

11. 'I'm really ___ that new series on Channel 4.' 'Me too! I can't stop watching it.'
    - a on
    - b out of
    - c into
    - d out

12. Mark didn't go to the match. He's not a big fan ___ football.
    - a with
    - b in
    - c for
    - d of

13. The USA became ___ from Britain in 1776.
    - a relaxing
    - b confident
    - c independent
    - d creative

14. You can see the world when you ___ the seas.
    - a dive
    - b swim
    - c cycle
    - d sail

15. Mike kicked the ball hard, but the ___ stopped him from scoring.
    - a goalkeeper
    - b manager
    - c fan
    - d referee

16. I used to ___ gymnastics when I was 10 years old.
    - a be
    - b make
    - c do
    - d go

17. 'Do you know a good place to ___ diving?' 'Yes, there's a place in the next town.'
    - a go
    - b do
    - c take
    - d have

18. I need a new bat for the ___ match.
    - a tennis
    - b football
    - c cricket
    - d basketball

19. 'Can I borrow your ___ to play tennis?' 'Of course.'
    - a court
    - b pitch
    - c net
    - d racket

20. That gym has a great ___ for basketball.
    - a pitch
    - b pool
    - c field
    - d court

Grammar

B Choose the correct answers.

1 If you put water in the freezer, it ___ into ice.
 a turning c turns
 b turned   d turn

2 I'm sure if you study, you ___ the exam.
 a passes   c pass
 b passed   d 'll pass

3 If we ___ to class early, we'll get good seats.
 a came   c will come
 b comes   d come

4 We ___ all the stars at night if we go to the countryside.
 a not see c see
 b saw   d can see

5 ___ is my favourite form of exercise.
 a To running c To run
 b Running   d Run

6 ___ me a ticket if you get to the theatre first?
 a Do you buy   c Will you buy
 b You buy   d You will buy

7 'What's wrong, John?'
 'I don't want ___ today.'
 a to practise   c practising
 b to practising   d practise

8 I hope ___ my exam this week.
 a will pass   c pass
 b to pass   d passing

9 She had better ___ on time for the show.
 a arrive   c to arrive
 b arriving d arrived

10 'I'm not into books, but I think art is exciting.'
 'I agree. I ___ rather paint than read.'
 a will   c could
 b had   d would

11 '___ I join a swimming club?'
 'Yes, that's a good idea.'
 a Shall   c Should
 b May   d Would

12 'Are we allowed to go inside?'
 'Yes, you ___.'
 a can   c must
 b would   d should

13 You ___ leave the house without your jacket. It's cold and raining.
 a shall   c can't
 b wouldn't d must

14 He ___ run 20 kilometres when he was a student.
 a used   c would
 b can   d could

15 'What advice can you give me about guitar lessons?'
 'You ___ have a lesson at least three times a week.'
 a may   c should
 b will   d can

16 You ___ put your hand on the cooker. It's really hot.
 a needn't c mustn't
 b can't   d must

17 We ___ to study for the maths exam. It has been cancelled.
 a mustn't c needn't
 b have   d don't have

18 You ___ have a drawing lesson before you can do the painting class.
 a have to c don't have
 b need   d will

19 We ___ bring any lunch on the trip. Food is included.
 a have to   c must
 b needn't   d need

20 I didn't do well on this exam, but I ___ get an A on the next one.
 a need   c shall
 b would   d should

Review 4 Units 7 & 8 59

9 Take a Break

Reading

A Read the *Exam Reminder*. What option should you choose if you can't find the answer in the text?

_____

B Now complete the *Exam Task*.

Exam Reminder

Checking for enough information
- Some tasks have 'Doesn't say' in the answer options. You choose this option when there isn't enough information in the text to choose the 'Right' or 'Wrong' options.
- Try to find specific information in the text that relates to what the question is asking. If it's not there, 'Doesn't say' is the answer.

To: Barney
From: Lille
Greetings from Hawaii

Hi Barney,

How's it going? How is your holiday? I thought I'd write you an email to find out about your holiday, and of course, to tell you about mine!

Hawaii is a really amazing place. It took us a really long time to get here from England – 30 hours! But I'm glad I came. We're staying on the Big Island, which has volcanoes. You can visit them and watch them erupt. It's such a special experience. Who can say they've seen a volcano erupt? I couldn't until now! The weather has been a bit strange lately, and it almost reminds me of England. It's quite cloudy, but definitely warmer. We've been to Punalu'u Beach, which has black sand, and tomorrow we're going sightseeing round Hilo, the island's capital.

Tell me all about your holiday! Where did you decide to go? Where are you staying? What are the sights?

Bye for now,

Lille

To: Lille
From: Barney
RE: Greetings from Hawaii

Hi Lille,

Thanks so much for your email. It's good to hear from you. It's great to be on summer holiday, isn't it?

Things are fantastic here in Norway. The weather is amazing. It's been so sunny. I don't think it's as warm as Hawaii. Actually, at night it's a bit cold, but I don't mind. The area we are in is awesome. We're near the coast, and we're staying in a cottage that belongs to my grandma. She doesn't usually live here, as she has a flat in Oslo. She's coming here in a couple of days.

We've done a few things since we've been here, such as camping in the woods behind my grandma's cottage. We're hoping to see the Northern Lights, which I've never experienced. We have to go a long way to see them, though, but I think it will be interesting.

Well, that's all for now. When do you return from holiday? We get back at the end of the month. I'll see you then!

Talk to you soon,

Barney

Exam Task

Read the emails written by two teenagers. Are sentences 1–8 'Right' (**A**) or 'Wrong' (**B**)? If there is not enough information to answer 'Right' (**A**) or 'Wrong' (**B**), choose 'Doesn't say' (**C**).

1. Lille travelled for more than one day to get to Hawaii.
2. Lille has seen a volcano erupt before this trip.
3. The weather was exactly like England's during Lille's stay.
4. Lille plans to visit other Hawaiian islands.
5. Barney is unhappy about the cold nights in Norway.
6. A member of Barney's family lives in Norway.
7. Barney and his family have visited Oslo.
8. Barney has seen the Northern Lights.

Vocabulary

A Write which continent these groups of countries belong to.

1. China, Thailand, India and Mongolia _____
2. Switzerland, Italy, Denmark and Poland _____
3. Peru, Argentina, Colombia and Chile _____
4. Egypt, South Africa, Morocco and Chad _____
5. the USA, Canada and Mexico _____
6. Australia, New Zealand and Fiji _____

B Complete the words in the sentences.

1. A c _ _ _ _ _ _ _ is place where people can put up their tents.
2. Some people sometimes stay in a y _ _ _ _ h _ _ _ _ _ _ because it's cheap.
3. After their wedding, the couple booked a room at a lovely b _ _ and b _ _ _ _ _ _ _ _ _.
4. Joseph and his family stayed in an Italian v _ _ _ _ with a view of Lake Como.

C Complete the text with these words.

agents   guide   parks   resorts   tourist   weekend

My dad likes planning holidays his own way. He doesn't like holiday (1) _____ because they're too full of people. He won't go to see travel (2) _____ because he doesn't like their advice. He never stops at (3) _____ information centres because he says they often give out the wrong information! So we have a caravan, and we stay at caravan (4) _____ and cook and eat there. It's fun, but I always wish we could do something else for a change.

So last month I asked him to take us to Edinburgh for a long (5) _____. We drove there, which took a few hours. We hired a tour (6) _____ to show us the sights. I thought, 'Oh, Dad's going to hate it,' but actually, they really got on well. I'm glad my dad finally enjoyed normal holiday stuff.

An image of Edinburgh Castle, Scotland

Take a Break 9

D Circle the correct words.

1 Did you live / take / stay a holiday when school finished?
2 We were so tired after walking round Madrid, but it was great to take / stay / see all the sights.
3 Hurry up and take / pack / stay your bags; we're leaving for the airport in 30 minutes!
4 I don't like seeing / wondering / taking photos on holiday; I don't want to carry a camera around with me all day.
5 We wandered / saw / stayed along the beach all morning.
6 How many more days are we going to live / stay / take at this hotel? It's awful!

E Match the words to the photos.

amusement park   passport   sunglasses   surfing

F Read the *Exam Reminder* and complete the *Exam Task*.

Exam Task

Read the descriptions of some words about travelling. What is the word for each one? The first letter is already there. There is one space for each other letter in the word.

1 If you travel to a country for a holiday, you are this. t _ _ _ _ _ _
2 People often stay in one of these while on holiday. h _ _ _ _
3 If you want to write to your friends and show them where you are, send them this. p _ _ _ _ _ _ _
4 This is when you pay someone to show you round a place and tell you about it. g _ _ _ _ _ t _ _ _
5 When you visit a large town for a short period of time, you're having this. c _ _ _ b _ _ _ _

Exam Reminder

Looking for clues
- Try to find clues, or key words, in the sentences that describe the words you're looking for.
- A clue can tell you if the missing word is a person, place, thing, activity, etc.
- Don't forget that you will have the first letter of the word and you will know how many letters the word has.

9 Take a Break

Grammar

Relative Pronouns; Adverbs

A Circle the correct words.

1 My aunt lives in a house that / who is red and blue.
2 My mum's mum is the grandmother who / – lives with us.
3 London is the city who / which I have visited the most.
4 That's the travel agent – / that is on the poster.
5 This is the guide book who / – I used in Spain.
6 Venice is a great city for parents whom / who have young children.

B Complete the text with one word in each gap. Sometimes more than one answer is possible.

Where would you like to go?

I have two friends (1) _____ have travelled to the Himalayas. The Himalayas are the mountains (2) _____ are the tallest in the world, but my friends didn't climb them, of course. Mark and James are friends (3) _____ I've known all my life, and they are both just 14 years old. They went there with Mark's dad, but they were too young to climb the mountains. Some people (4) _____ aren't good climbers go to these mountains and try to climb them, but they have problems. So Mark and James didn't climb. They did, however, hire a tour guide. The people (5) _____ live in the area and give guided tours are called Sherpas. The Sherpas (6) _____ Mark and James' family hired have lived in the Himalayas all their lives, and so did their parents and grandparents. The Sherpas know how dangerous the mountains can be. They use equipment (7) _____ is the best in the world for exploring the area. Mark and James had a great time. Because of their stories, this is the place (8) _____ I want to visit the most!

A beautiful view of the Himalayan mountains, Nepal

C Read the *Exam Reminder* and complete the *Exam Task*.

Exam Reminder

Choosing the correct word type

- Often, multiple-choice options look alike. In these cases, you have to decide what type of word you need. Read the whole sentence to find out what kind of word the gap needs.
- Word endings can help you identify what type of word each answer option is. You may see *-ly* endings for adverbs, and *-er* and *-est* endings for comparative and superlative adjectives.
- When a gap needs a relative pronoun, find out what noun it refers to to help you choose your answer.

Exam Task

Read the email about a day trip. Choose the best word (**a**, **b** or **c**) for each space.

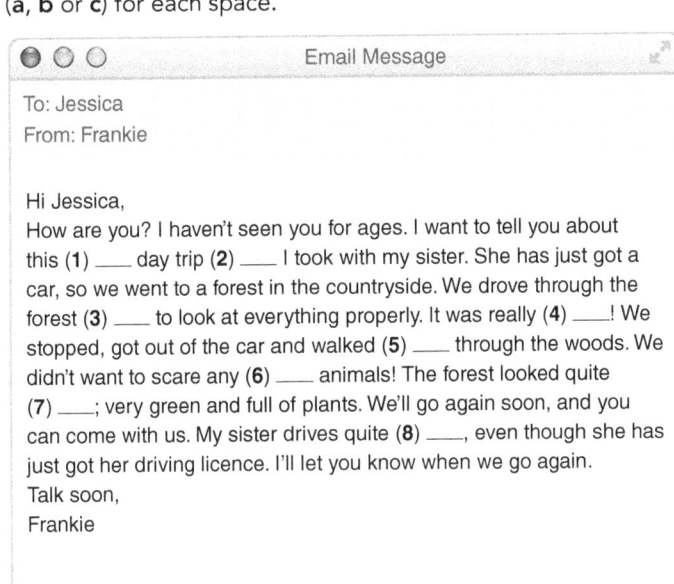

Hi Jessica,
How are you? I haven't seen you for ages. I want to tell you about this (1) ___ day trip (2) ___ I took with my sister. She has just got a car, so we went to a forest in the countryside. We drove through the forest (3) ___ to look at everything properly. It was really (4) ___! We stopped, got out of the car and walked (5) ___ through the woods. We didn't want to scare any (6) ___ animals! The forest looked quite (7) ___; very green and full of plants. We'll go again soon, and you can come with us. My sister drives quite (8) ___, even though she has just got her driving licence. I'll let you know when we go again.
Talk soon,
Frankie

1 a amazingly   b amaze   c amazing
2 a which   b who   c whose
3 a slowly   b slow   c fast
4 a beauty   b beautiful   c beautifully
5 a careful   b care   c carefully
6 a hungry   b hungrily   c angrily
7 a healthier   b healthily   c healthy
8 a good   b well   c better

Take a Break **9**

D Complete the sentences with the correct form of the words in brackets.

1 Jim was happy to see his friend, and he shouted _____ to get his attention. **LOUD**
2 Michelle looked _____ when she found out her friend lied to her. **ANGRY**
3 Martin asked the teacher _____ if she could help him with his homework. **POLITE**
4 The train travelled so _____ that they arrived in Paris in less than an hour. **FAST**
5 Monica felt _____ that she forgot to invite her friend on the trip. **BAD**
6 They welcomed their guests _____ when they got to the house. **WARM**

Listening

A Read the *Exam Reminder*. How many speakers will there be in each conversation?

_____

B 9.1 ▶ Listen and complete the *Exam Task*.

> **Exam Reminder**
>
> **Getting ready to listen**
> - Look at the pictures before you begin. What is similar or different about them?
> - We can often predict the content of conversations. You can do that by looking at the pictures and thinking about what the speakers will talk about.
> - The speakers are usually one male and one female. Because there are only two speakers, you can easily follow what they say.

Exam Task

You will hear five short conversations. You will hear each conversation twice. There is one question for each conversation. For each question, choose the right answer (**a**, **b** or **c**).

1 Which continent is the man visiting?

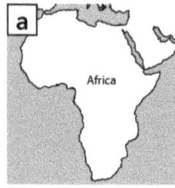 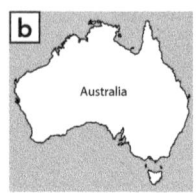 
a Africa   b Australia   c South America

2 How long are the couple going on holiday for?

a   b   c

3 Where is the boy going to stay?

a   b   c

4 When is Natalie's flight?

 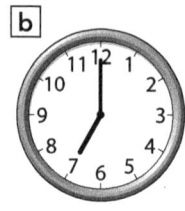 
a   b   c

5 How did John feel on his holiday?

 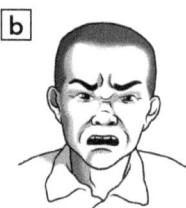 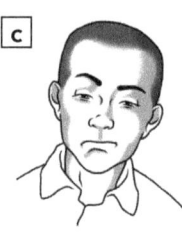
a   b   c

C 9.2 ▶ Listen again and check your answers.

Writing: a social media post

Learning Reminder

Making your writing flow
- For your writing to be easy to read, each sentence of a paragraph must connect to the next one smoothly.
- To help do this and make your writing more interesting for your reader, make sure you don't repeat the same words too often. Try to use different words.

A Rewrite these sentences so that they flow more smoothly.

1 I've been in Spain for a week now. Spain is a great place. It's great to be here.
   _____

2 Our guided tour yesterday was quite fun. We went on a guided tour to Machu Picchu. Machu Picchu is an amazing place!
   _____

3 I'm quite disappointed in Venice. In Venice, the weather is very rainy. That's very disappointing.
   _____

B Read the writing task below and then correct the mistakes in the sentences.

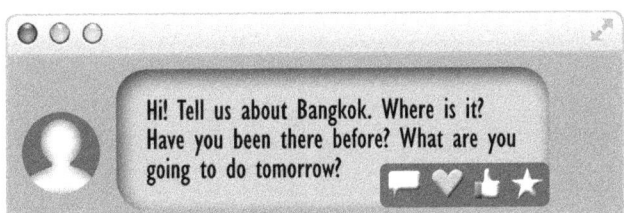

Read the social media post from your friend, Philip. Write a post for your social media page and answer the questions. Write 25–35 words.

1 You should write an email.
   _____

2 You will write about what you did yesterday.
   _____

3 Philip is in Bangkok.
   _____

C Read the example social media post. Correct the punctuation mistakes.

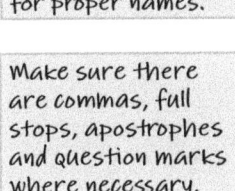

Use capital letters for proper names.

Make sure there are commas, full stops, apostrophes and question marks where necessary.

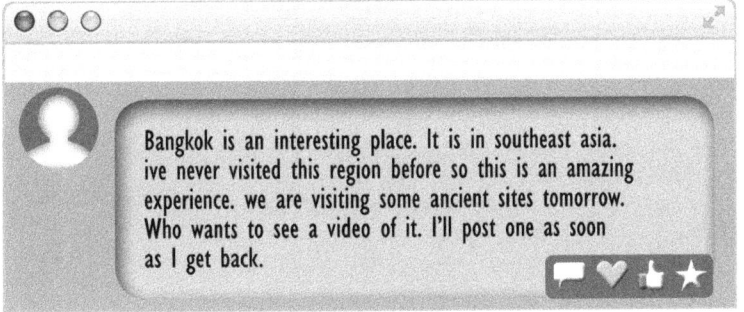

Bangkok is an interesting place. It is in southeast asia. ive never visited this region before so this is an amazing experience. we are visiting some ancient sites tomorrow. Who wants to see a video of it. I'll post one as soon as I get back.

Remember to check the punctuation in your text carefully.

D Read and complete the *Exam Task* below. Don't forget to use the *Useful Expressions* on page 119 of your Student's Book.

Exam Task

Read the post on a social media site from your friend, Shannon.

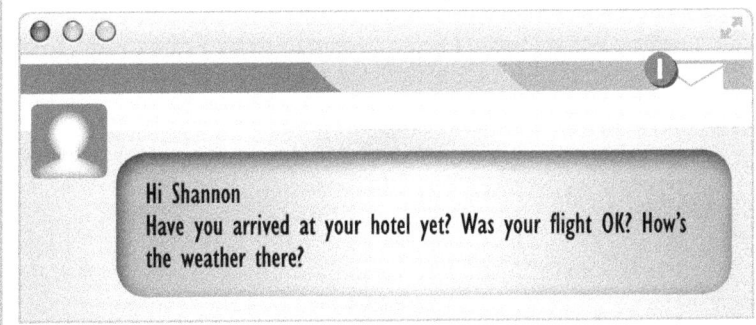

Hi Shannon
Have you arrived at your hotel yet? Was your flight OK? How's the weather there?

Write a post for your social media page and answer the questions. Write 25–35 words.

Take a Break **9**

10 Road Trip!

Reading

A Read the *Exam Reminder*. What word has a similar meaning to *go out*?

_____

B Now complete the *Exam Task*.

Exam Reminder

Looking for words with similar meanings
- Sometimes the notices have words with similar meanings to the words in the sentences. Look for matching words and phrases as soon as you begin the task.
- Some examples are *go in* and *enter*, *go out* and *exit*, *leave* and *depart*, *get on* and *board*, etc. You may not know the whole meaning of the sentence or sign, but if you can match words together, you may find the right answer.

Exam Task

Which notice (A–H) says this (1–5)?

1. You cannot pass here because it's unsafe. ☐
2. Get your bags here after you travel. ☐
3. Use this if there are accidents or other difficulties. ☐
4. You need to show your travel papers. ☐
5. People are fixing the street, so you mustn't go fast. ☐

A

Pull handle in case of emergencies.

B
Please keep hands inside train at all times.

C
Passport control

– please have your passport ready

D
NO PARKING
– passenger loading and unloading only

E
Road work ahead
– please drive slowly

F
Danger!
Do not cross train tracks.

G
Luggage reclaim area

H
Low bridge
0.5 kilometres ahead
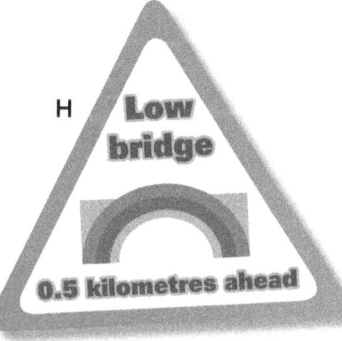

C Read the article. Which signs from B might you see in or near the type of building in the article?

Going nowhere!

Our travel plans can often change. It happens because of events that we can't predict, such as bad weather, traffic and illness. Unbelievably, sometimes even a travel route that was once popular completely disappears. This happened to the train station in Canfranc, Spain. It's a train station in which no passengers enter and no passengers leave. It's a shame because the station is beautiful. It's high in the Pyrenees mountains, at almost 1,200 metres above sea level. It's nearly a quarter of a kilometre long and has got 300 windows and 156 doors. It opened in 1928 and it connected towns in southern France and northern Spain. The Spanish king and the French president of the time were present during the opening. In 1970, a train bridge on the French side was destroyed. The French decided not to build another bridge, so the station closed. You can go on a guided tour of the station in the summer, but don't expect to travel through it by train!

Canfranc International Railway Station, Spain

Vocabulary

A Circle the correct words.

1 We need to look at a timetable / passenger to find out when the train leaves.
2 My car hasn't got any gear / petrol, so we can't go anywhere.
3 Michael didn't take a lorry / taxi because he didn't have enough money to pay the driver.
4 The children wanted to meet the pilot / captain of the ship to learn about his job.
5 The queue / motorway was full of traffic, and Adele was really late for work.
6 When the ship arrived at the port / platform, everyone hurried to get off.

B Circle the odd word out.

1	plane	airport	road	ticket
2	train	platform	timetable	pilot
3	helicopter	sail	port	ship
4	rickshaw	reed boat	electric car	coach

C Complete the conversations with these words.

adult's   destination   fare   return

1 **A:** The _____ is £7.50. Here's your ticket.
   B: Thank you.
2 **A:** Can I change my ticket? I bought a child's ticket instead of an _____ ticket.
   B: Don't worry. I can change the ticket for you.
3 **A:** Are you going to Toledo?
   B: No, I have to get another train when I get there. My final _____ is Zaragoza.
4 **A:** Isn't it cheaper to get a single ticket than a _____ ticket?
   B: No, it isn't. Surprisingly, they are the same price!

D Complete the text with these words and phrases.

bus stop   caught   ferry   journey   lose   miss

I once visited the island of Jersey for a long weekend. The (1) _____ there was interesting because of all things that went wrong. First, I walked to the (2) _____ and waited for the bus to take me to the port. I had my ticket for the (3) _____ that goes to the island, which I bought the day before, so I was ready to go. It was raining heavily – not a good day to travel. There was a lot of water on the road, and when the bus came, it splashed all over me! I had to wait an hour and twenty minutes for the bus, and I thought I might (4) _____ the boat because it was leaving in 45 minutes. I got to the port with five minutes left. I looked for the ticket, but I couldn't find it. How could I (5) _____ a ticket so easily? So I had to buy another, but I (6) _____ the boat and I got to Jersey and the weather was sunny. There was not a drop of rain in sight!

E Choose the correct answers.

1 I bought a ___ ticket to Berlin because I wasn't sure how long I was staying.
   a single   b double   c return
2 In ___ class, you get special drinks and meals, but it will be expensive.
   a regular   b standard   c first
3 My son is only six years old, so I'd like a(n) ___ fare for him.
   a adult's   b cash   c child's
4 I paid for my ticket ___ because I didn't have enough money in my purse for the fare.
   a with £20   b by card   c in cash

F Match the first parts of the sentences 1–7 to the second parts a–g.

1 My flight leaves at 3 pm, so can you drop me   a up at 2.30?
2 It was a nice day, so I got   b in the taxi as quickly as possible.
3 My flight arrives at 2 pm, so can you pick me   c off at 2.30?
4 Michael thought Paul was in the car, and he drove   d on it.
5 It was raining heavily, so I got   e out of the car and buying the ticket for the car park.
6 The train was leaving, so I had to run to get   f off the bus and walked.
7 Do you mind getting   g off without him.

G Complete the sentences with one word in each gap.

1 It's getting late; shall I _____ a taxi to take you home?
2 You'd better start running if you want to _____ that bus!
3 It's fun to _____ a motorbike.
4 It takes weeks of lessons to learn how to _____ a plane.
5 My dad learned how to _____ a boat in the Andaman Sea.
6 I would like to _____ a car across the country one day.
7 My jacket is completely _____, so I don't need to worry about the rain.
8 Can you give me a _____ with these bags? There are so many of them!

10 Road Trip!

Grammar

The Passive Voice: Present Simple; The Passive Voice: Past Simple

A Complete the sentences with the Present Simple passive form of the verbs in brackets.

1. The bus _____ (**drive**) by an experienced driver.
2. Planes _____ (**fly**) in bad weather all the time.
3. These days, most plane tickets _____ (**buy**) online.
4. I'm sorry, but food and drinks _____ (**not serve**) on this short flight.
5. The bus you're waiting for _____ (**usually delay**) because of traffic.
6. This airport _____ (**not use**) by helicopters.

B Rewrite these sentences in the Present Simple passive form.

1. Thousands of people visit this wall.
   _____
2. They closed the ticket office for the moment.
   _____
3. Storms never scare the pilots.
   _____
4. They check your passport at passport control.
   _____
5. They usually put timetables in the information centre.
   _____
6. We don't leave mobile phones on during flights.
   _____

C Complete the sentences with these words in the Past Simple passive form.

   build   film   hide   send   steal   write

1. It took a few hours to find my keys because they _____ by my brother.
2. This airport _____ by a famous architect in 1956.
3. I'm sorry, but the letters _____ to the wrong address.
4. I'm so upset! My bike _____ last night.
5. Did you see whom the emails _____ to?
6. Where _____ this holiday video _____?

D Write questions for these answers with the Past Simple passive form and the words in brackets.

1. It was taken in a park in Tokyo. (**this photo**)
   _____
2. It was sent by my sister. (**this email**)
   _____
3. They were bought on Wednesday. (**these flowers**)
   _____
4. It was made using wood from India. (**this chair**)
   _____
5. It was cooked yesterday. (**this cake**)
   _____
6. I was given it by my mum. (**this necklace**)
   _____

Road Trip! **10**

E Choose the correct answers.

Barra Airport (1) ___ in the Outer Hebrides of Scotland, and it's unusual because it's on a beach. The planes land right on top of sand. The airport (2) ___ in 1936 and it (3) ___ by small planes. A normal landing area (4) ___ because light planes can take off and land easily from the sand. It does get quite windy at Barra. Once, the weather was so bad that the luggage area (5) ___ and all of the suitcases (6) ___ across the beach.

An airplane preparing for take off on the sandy runway of Barra Airport, Scotland

	a	b	c
1	located	was located	is located
2	is opened	was opened	were opened
3	are only used	only used	is only used
4	was created	was never created	is created
5	destroyed	is destroyed	was destroyed
6	were blown	are blown	was blown

Listening

A Read the *Exam Reminder*. What should you do if you make a mistake?

_____

B 10.1 Listen and complete the *Exam Task*.

Exam Task

You will hear a woman asking a man about a guided tour. Listen and complete each question. You will hear the conversation twice.

Beijing Tours

Place: Great Wall of China

Walking tour lasts: (1) _____ hours

Leave from: Royal Hotel at (2) _____ am

Traditional Chinese lunch at a (3) _____ near the wall

The part of the wall near Beijing is (4) _____ km long.

Price per person: (5) £ _____

Exam Reminder

Predicting the answers before listening

- Look at the gaps and decide what information would go in each gap before you play the recording.
- Imagine how the speakers will talk about that missing information. For example, for a gap that needs a ticket price, you might hear 'How much did you pay for your ticket?'
- Make sure each gap has only one answer. If you make a mistake, put a line through the answer that you don't want.

C 10.2 Listen again and check your answers.

A section of the Great Wall of China, Jinshanling

Writing: an invitation

Learning Reminder

Using modals

- We use modal verbs when we invite people to do things and when we reply to an invitation. For example, we ask *Would you like to come to my party?* and we reply *I would really like to come* to accept or *I'm sorry, but I can't come* to decline. The modal verbs here are *would* and *can't*.
- We also use modal verbs to make offers (*shall*), to ask for and give permission (*could*, *may* and *can*) and to ask for and give advice (*should*). Learn the structure of modals so that your writing is polite and uses the correct English grammar.

A Decide if the sentences are making an invitation, making an offer, asking for permission or asking for advice.

1 Should I go on holiday to Scotland in the summer?
   _____

2 Can I borrow your leather jacket for my trip to Sweden?
   _____

3 Would you like to join me for lunch this afternoon?
   _____

4 Shall I look after your pets while you're away?
   _____

B Read the writing task below and then decide if the sentences are true (T) or false (F).

Email Message

Hi,
Would you like to go to the museum with me on Sunday? I want to go about 12 and maybe we could do something else after. Should we invite Marcia? Also, can I borrow your notes from the history lesson? Let me know.

Read the email from your friend, Jarrod.
Write an email to Jarrod and answer the questions. Write 25–35 words.

1 You should write an email to Marcia. ☐
2 You should answer Jarrod's questions. ☐
3 The email is making an offer. ☐

C Read the example email and complete it with these modal verbs.

`can   can't   shall   should   would`

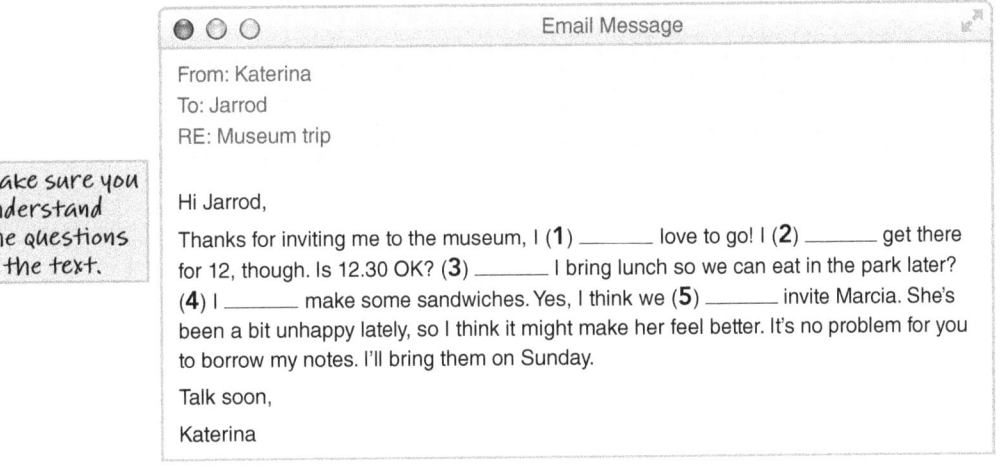

Email Message

From: Katerina
To: Jarrod
RE: Museum trip

Hi Jarrod,

Thanks for inviting me to the museum. I (**1**) _____ love to go! I (**2**) _____ get there for 12, though. Is 12.30 OK? (**3**) _____ I bring lunch so we can eat in the park later? (**4**) I _____ make some sandwiches. Yes, I think we (**5**) _____ invite Marcia. She's been a bit unhappy lately, so I think it might make her feel better. It's no problem for you to borrow my notes. I'll bring them on Sunday.

Talk soon,
Katerina

Make sure you understand the questions in the text.

Look for modal verbs in the sentences. They tell you the function of the question or sentence.

Understanding the function is important to help you respond correctly.

D Read and complete the *Exam Task* below. Don't forget to use the *Useful Expressions* on page 131 of your Student's Book.

Exam Task

Email Message

From: Melissa
Trip

I'm having a party on Saturday at 7 pm to celebrate the end of the exams. Would you like to come? If so, can you bring some snacks and drinks? Also, will you help me decorate my living room before the party?
Melissa

Read the email from your friend, Melissa.
Write an email to Melissa and answer the questions. Write 25–35 words.

▶ Writing Reference p. 173 in Student's Book

Road Trip! **10**

Review 5

Vocabulary

A Choose the correct answers.

1. 'Have you been to China?'
   'No. In fact, I've never been to ___.'
   a South America   c Asia
   b North America   d Africa

2. France is one of the largest countries in ___.
   a Europe   c South America
   b Asia   d Oceania

3. This ___ is a great cheap place for students.
   a caravan   c villa
   b bedroom   d youth hostel

4. 'What are you doing for the long ___.'
   'I'm going to stay at home and sleep!'
   a centre   c weekend
   b guide   d resort

5. What sights did you ___ in Madrid?
   a hear   c look
   b say   d see

6. We hired a tour ___ to show us the town.
   a agent   c book
   b bag   d guide

7. We ___ around the streets of Rome until the evening.
   a stayed   c wandered
   b lived   d wondered

8. The ___ guide knew a lot about the history of the town.
   a tour   c excursion
   b travel   d trip

9. I'm sending a ___ to a friend to show her where I am.
   a guide   c passport
   b suitcase   d postcard

10. 'Can you help me ___ my bags?'
    'Of course.'
    a create   c pack
    b do   d make

11. 'It's late. How should I get home?'
    'Don't worry. I'll call a ___.'
    a ferry   c plane
    b helicopter   d taxi

12. Gondolas are a very ___ form of transport in Venice.
    a waterproof   c guided
    b weird   d popular

13. 'This train doesn't go to Milan.'
    'You're right. We're on the wrong ___.'
    a timetable   c driver
    b ticket   d platform

14. Many people have their driving ___ by the time they're 18.
    a engineer   c diploma
    b licence   d mechanic

15. 'How much is the ___ to London?'
    'Twelve pounds, sir.'
    a standard   c fare
    b adult   d destination

16. Keep your passport with you at all times. Don't ___ it.
    a miss   c pass
    b lose   d give

17. When Hank reached his stop, he quickly got ___ the train.
    a off   c on
    b out   d into

18. 'I'm afraid I can't take you to the gym.'
    'That's OK. I'll ___ the bus.'
    a grab   c catch
    b do   d go

19. Can you pick me ___ in your car when my class finishes?
    a at   c up
    b out   d off

20. Let's go ___ class to Monaco. I don't care how much it costs!
    a return   c standard
    b first   d coach

Grammar

B Choose the correct answers.

1. Is that the woman ___ lives across from you?
   a whom   c who
   b –   d which

2. 'What did this old building use to be?'
   'It was the school ___ I used to attend.'
   a this   c –
   b what   d who

3. That's my daughter's friend ___ I drove to school once.
   a this   c her
   b she   d whom

4. Monica ___ opened her presents on her birthday.
   a happily   c happiest
   b happy   d happier

5. He finished his homework so ___ that he made lots of mistakes.
   a quick   c hard
   b fast   d good

6. 'How was the performance?'
   'I don't think I did very ___.'
   a better   c well
   b fine   d good

7. 'Nick is a talented painter.'
   'I agree. He paints ___.'
   a more beautiful   c beautiful
   b beautifully   d beauty

8. They ate a ___ supper, then they went to bed.
   a healthier   c healthy
   b health   d healthily

9. I asked the waiter ___ if we could have lunch outside.
   a deep   c politely
   b polite   d deeply

10. Don't worry about the road. I'm a ___ driver.
    a more carefully   c careful
    b care   d carefully

11. Dinner ___ at 7 pm sharp.
    a serves   c served
    b is served   d serve

12. The hotel rooms ___ every day at 12 pm.
    a are cleaning   c are cleaned
    b is cleaned   d cleaned

13. The plane is flown ___ a skilled pilot.
    a using   c with
    b in   d by

14. What kind of films ___ most often at this cinema?
    a are shown   c show
    b is shown   d shows

15. 'Where is Skara Brae?'
    'It ___ in northern Scotland.'
    a will locate   c located
    b is located   d locates

16. 'How old is this church?'
    'It ___ in 1592.'
    a were built   c built
    b is built   d was built

17. I love the colour of your house. ___ painted by a professional?
    a Was it   c Were they
    b It was   d They were

18. 'Where were ___?'
    'In Italy.'
    a made these clothes   c these clothes make
    b these clothes   d these clothes made

19. 'What happened to your camera?'
    'It ___ on holiday.'
    a were stolen   c is stolen
    b was stolen   d was stealing

20. 'Who picked up your kids from school?'
    'Their grandma ___ them up.'
    a was picked   c picks
    b picked   d is picked

Review 5 Units 9 & 10   73

11 It's Raining Cats & Dogs

Reading

A Read the *Exam Reminder*. What should you look for in the reply if a question uses *where*?

_____

B Now complete the *Exam Task*.

Exam Reminder

Understanding questions
- It is important to understand questions in order to find the correct replies.
- Make sure you underline the question words. If they're *Wh-* questions, the replies must match the question words. For example, for *who*, look for a person's name in the replies. Don't forget that *how often*, *how much* and *how many* are also question words.
- For yes/no questions, look for *yes*, *no* or something similar in the replies to find the right answer.

Exam Task

Part 1

Complete the five conversations. Choose **a**, **b** or **c**.

1. How's the weather in Madrid today?
   a It was really windy yesterday.
   b It usually rains a lot.
   c It's quite warm and sunny.
2. How often do you have storms in your area?
   a I can't get to school when we have storms.
   b It happens a lot in spring.
   c It's often very cold in spring.
3. What will the weather be like for your holiday?
   a I think it will be perfect.
   b We'll be gone for a week.
   c It was quite warm the last time we went.
4. Did you see the weather report for tomorrow?
   a I hope it doesn't rain.
   b No, I missed it, unfortunately.
   c Yes, it's going to be quite cloudy next week.
5. We can't go skiing because there's no snow.
   a What a shame!
   b I can't wait!
   c How much snow is there?

Part 2

Complete the conversation between two classmates. What does Alisha say to Roger? Choose the correct answer **A–H**. There are three letters you do not need to use.

Roger: The rain outside looks terrible, doesn't it?
Alisha: (6) ___
Roger: How will you get home from school?
Alisha: (7) ___
Roger: That's good. I usually walk home, but today I may get the bus.
Alisha: (8) ___
Roger: No, that's OK. Thanks for the offer, though. Do you have an umbrella I could borrow?
Alisha: (9) ___
Roger: Thanks so much! I can stay dry while I wait for the bus. I'll bring it back tomorrow.
Alisha: (10) ___
Roger: I have one at home, too. If it rains tomorrow, I'll bring both to school!

A It's supposed to rain all day.
B Actually, my dad is picking me up.
C Would you like to come with us?
D I hope you get home from school OK.
E It certainly does!
F Why don't you buy an umbrella?
G Yes, I do. I'll get it for you.
H No problem! I have another at home, anyway.

C Read the article. Which conversation in B, Part 1 applies to the article?

Man-made weather
In most places in the Middle East, it's hot almost all year round and it hardly ever rains. The city of Dubai, however, is home to the largest indoor ski centre, where there's plenty of snow and cold weather for everyone. The temperature indoors never rises higher than –4°C during the day. That's incredible because it is often 40°C outdoors. The indoor mountain is 85 metres high, and the ski slope is 400 metres long. The centre has an ice cave, and there are even penguins to play with! It's a small piece of winter in a place you wouldn't expect.

Vocabulary

A Look at the pictures and complete the sentences.

We've got some _____ weather at the moment.

Those hilltops are quite _____!

There's _____ all over the ground.

The skies are very _____ at the moment.

It's quite _____ and warm today.

It's so _____ that you can barely walk!

B Match the dates to the correct season.

1 spring ☐
2 summer ☐
3 autumn ☐
4 winter ☐

a 22nd of January
b 12th of August
c 24th of April
d 1st of November

C Complete the words in the sentences.

1 It snowed in the mountains all night, so today's a great day to go s _ _ _ _ _ _.
2 Some of my plants in the garden have died because of this terrible d _ _ _ _ _ _.
3 Did you hear that loud t _ _ _ _ _ _? It's going to rain soon.
4 Mary's kitchen floor was covered in water because of a f _ _ _ _.
5 There's a b _ _ _ f _ _ _ near the campsite, and that's why we can see smoke.
6 The l _ _ _ _ _ _ _ _ during the storm was very scary.

It's Raining Cats & Dogs **11**

D Complete the online chat with these words.

boiling   cloudy   cool   freezing   how's   ice   like   warm

Glen: What's the weather (1) _____ in Melbourne at the moment?

Sherry: Oh, it's (2) _____. I can't go out without a heavy coat on. (3) _____ the weather in London?

Glen: It's quite (4) _____, about 28°C. The skies are a bit (5) _____, but the sun comes out occasionally.

Sherry: Well, we're having our winter, which is your summer. It rained the other day, and it was so cold, the rain turned to (6) _____ on the pavement. It was difficult to walk!

Glen: Well, the weather's nice here at the moment, but it's going to be (7) _____ next week. They're saying it will be over 32°C!

Sherry: You should stay in a (8) _____ place when that happens.

Glen: I will!

E Read the *Exam Reminder* and complete the *Exam Task*.

Exam Task

Complete the text about a dry place. Write ONE word for each space.

The Atacama Desert

The Atacama is a desert (1) _____ South America. It (2) _____ known as the driest place on earth. There are long periods where there is little or (3) _____ rain. Anyone who visits the Atacama must bring plenty (4) _____ water. It only rains about 15 millimetres a year, with a few places receiving much less. In fact, some weather stations in the Atacama have never had (5) _____ rain. The area has been a desert (6) _____ three million years. This means the Atacama may be (7) _____ oldest desert on earth. (8) _____ doesn't this desert ever get any rain? It is (9) _____ two mountain ranges – the Andes to the north and the Chilean Coast Range to the south. It's such a dry place that people have said it looks (10) _____ Mars!

Exam Reminder

Deciding what kind of word is missing

- Missing words can be a part of phrases, collocations or grammatical structures. Look at the words around the gap to see what phrase or tense is in the sentence to help you decide on the missing word.
- Gaps can also come before nouns. In these cases, think of articles and adjectives that may work in the gap.

The sun setting on the Atacama Desert, Chile

11 It's Raining Cats & Dogs

Grammar

Comparative Adjectives; Comparative Adverbs; Superlative Adjectives; Superlative Adverbs

A Complete the sentences with the correct form of the words in brackets. Use the words *more*, *as* and *than* where needed.

1. Today's maths exam was a lot _____ (**hard**) than the one last week.
2. Michael is a good rugby player because he's _____ (**strong**) most of his teammates.
3. Getting lots of rain is _____ (**good**) than having no rain at all.
4. My computer doesn't work as _____ (**fast**) it used to.
5. The weather this afternoon is not _____ (**cold**) as it was this morning.
6. Becca walks a lot _____ (**slow**) than she did before she hurt her leg.

B Circle the correct words.

cold foggy heavy quick sunny warm

San Francisco has quite interesting weather. It's (**1**) warmer than / not so warm as some people might think, even in the summer. It's in California, but it's on the Pacific Ocean and it's much (**2**) colder / cold than the city of Los Angeles to the south. The amazing thing about San Francisco is the fog. The fog comes from the ocean, and because of that, the city is (**3**) foggier / as foggy than many other places in California. There's so much fog that many people want it to be (**4**) sunny / sunnier than it is! It's spectacular to see the fog pass over the city. It moves much (**5**) quicker / more quickly than normal clouds. You can see it pass through the city's skyscrapers and its famous Golden Gate Bridge. It also rains (**6**) more heavily / heavily than places in the south, so if you're looking for a suntan, go south!

Thick fog covering the Golden Gate Bridge in San Francisco

C Complete the sentences with the correct form of the words in brackets.

1. This spring was the _____ (**rainy**) one I've ever seen.
2. The weather today is the _____ (**good**) weather for skiing.
3. We had 16 centimetres of snow the other day, which was the _____ (**heavy**) we've had in a long time.
4. The _____ (**difficult**) part of being a weatherman is getting the forecast right.
5. The wind at the centre of a hurricane blows the _____ (**strong**).
6. The fire burnt the _____ (**bright**) in the middle of the forest.

D Circle the correct words.

1. I think today is colder / coldest than it was yesterday.
2. The 22nd of June is the longer / longest day of the year.
3. It started snowing the most / more heavily when I had to leave work.
4. The moon shines the most bright / brightly when it's a full moon.
5. The countryside is the most beautiful / beautifully in the spring.
6. We can agree that England is not the most sunny / sunniest place on earth.

It's Raining Cats & Dogs **11**

E Read the *Exam Reminder* and complete the *Exam Task*.

Exam Task

Complete the text about a windy place.
Write ONE word for each space.

Windy Wellington

Have you ever wondered which city in the world is (1) _____ windiest? The winds in Wellington, New Zealand are often 30 kilometres per hour. This makes the city (2) _____ than other famous cities such as Chicago and Edinburgh. On many days in Wellington, the winds are more (3) _____ 60 kilometres per hour. And on around 20 days a year, the wind speed can be as much (4) _____ 80 kilometres per hour. The fastest wind speed ever recorded was (5) _____ incredible 248 kilometres per hour! The reason they blow (6) _____ strongly here than anywhere else is because Wellington sits in the ocean between two large pieces of land. The winds get pushed through, and that creates the (7) _____ extreme winds in the world. How do people manage to live in this windy place? It's a very good city to live in – one of (8) _____ best places to live in the world, according to travel guides. So even though it's very windy there, the people are (9) _____ so upset about that (10) _____ you might think!

Exam Reminder

Writing the correct word

- Before you do the task, get a general understanding of the text by reading the title and the whole text first.
- Look at the words before and after the gaps to get clues, and make sure you write only one word and spell it correctly.

The Wellington Cable Car found in New Zealand

Listening

A Read the *Exam Reminder*. What word might you hear when people are talking about how hot or cold it is?

_____

B 11.1 ▶ Listen and complete the *Exam Task*.

Exam Task

You will hear a student tell their class about a recent holiday. Listen and complete each question. You will hear the information twice.

My holiday

Region visited: Mawsynram, in (1) _____ India

Temperature: (2) _____ degrees in the day

Interesting type of weather: very (3) _____ rainy season

Rainfall amount in 1985: (4) _____ centimetres

Fact about July: (5) _____ month of the year

Exam Reminder

Listening for numbers, adjectives & common words

- Certain numbers are followed by certain words. For example, temperatures are followed by *degrees*, distances are followed by *kilometres*, and so on.
- When you hear adjectives, remember to listen for reasons why that adjective is used.
- Learn how to spell common words, as the speaker will only spell unusual words.

C 11.2 ▶ Listen again and check your answers.

11 It's Raining Cats & Dogs

Writing: a postcard

A Circle the correct words.

1 Right now, I **write / am writing** to you from Malta.
2 We **went / have gone** swimming yesterday, which was fun.
3 Tomorrow, we **are going to / will** visit a nearby island.
4 I **have eaten / ate** so much since we arrived!
5 We **saw / have seen** all the important sights in town on the second day.
6 **Say / You say** hi to everyone back home!

Learning Reminder

Using a variety of tenses
- We often talk about things that happen at different times when we write postcards.
- Use the Present Continuous to talk about what you're doing at the moment, and the Past Simple to talk about things you did yesterday or the week before.
- Use the Present Perfect for things you've done. You can use words like *already* and *just* with the Present Perfect.
- Use *be going to* or the Present Continuous to talk about plans for the future.

B Read the writing task below and then circle the correct words in the sentences.

Read the task.

Imagine you are on a school exchange trip in another country. Write a postcard to your brother and tell him what you are doing, what you have done and what you are going to do before coming back home.

Write your postcard. Write between 40–50 words.

1 You **are / aren't** going to use past tenses in your postcard.
2 You **are / aren't** going to use future tenses in your postcard.
3 You **are / aren't** on holiday at the moment.

C Read the example postcard and complete it with the correct form of the verbs in brackets.

Think about what you want to say before you start.

Take a few minutes to plan your postcard.

Saturday, 2nd October

Hi Josh!

How are you? I thought I'd send you a postcard of beautiful Peru. At the moment, I (1) _____ (sit) in a café in busy Lima with a nice cup of coffee. I (2) _____ (have) such a great time since I arrived here last week. My home is close to school, so every day I (3) _____ (walk) there. Last weekend, my host family and I (4) _____ (travel) to Cusco, to see the historic centre. It's really lovely! Tomorrow, a classmate and I (5) _____ (visit) the prehistoric arts museum. Wish you were here!

Love,
Peggy

To: Josh Jones
14 Flower Rd
Oxford
OX21 4BF
UK

Make notes about what points you want to mention.

D Read and complete the Exam Task below. Don't forget to use the Useful Expressions on page 145 of your Student's Book.

Exam Task

Read the task.

Imagine you're an exchange student who's just moved to China. Write a postcard to your friend Paul and tell him what you are doing, what you have done during the week and what you're going to do next week.

Write your postcard. Write between 40–50 words.

▶ Writing Reference p. 174 in Student's Book

12 The World Around Us

Reading

A Read the *Exam Reminder*. When you look for specific information, do you need to read all of the text?

_____

B Now complete the *Exam Task*.

Exam Reminder

Looking for specific information
- You can find specific information in a text by looking for key words. You don't have to read the whole text.
- There are key words in the questions. Decide what those words are, find something similar in the text and you'll find the answers more quickly.

Going batty!

Jason Anderson **Date: 21st July**

So, for this blog I want to tell you about my love of bats, those furry creatures that fly around at night. I've learnt so many cool things about them, and I'd like to share what I've found out so far.

Did you know that bats fly around and eat lots of annoying insects? A bat can eat over 1,000 small insects in about an hour. I think you would need to to get enough food. It helps keep insects under control, so it's quite useful for us, too.

Another thing I recently learnt is that bats have amazing ears. They can hear an insect walking on the leaf of a tree. Isn't that incredible? But the poor insect doesn't know he's going to be a bat's dinner!

I've also learnt that some bats are so small they weigh about as much as a coin. That's the Kitti's hog-nosed bat, which lives in Southeast Asia. I'd like to see a bat like that. It's so small that I hope the other bats don't think it is an insect!

And I'm not the only one who loves bats. In Austin, Texas, there is a bridge that's home to 1.5 million bats. Tourists from all over the world come to see them fly when the sun goes down.

All of this makes me love bats even more. I was really happy to learn that there are organisations that protect them. In the UK, there are laws that stop people from harming them. That's really cool.

I hope you liked my blog entry this week. I posted a photo, too. It's good, isn't it? See you next week, when I visit a local cave. I hope to have a cool bat video to upload. Bye for now!

A dwarf fruit bat flying at night

Exam Task

Read the blog about bats. Choose the best answer (a, b or c) for each question.

1. In 60 minutes, a bat can
   a catch fewer than 1,000 insects.
   b eat more than 1,000 insects.
   c fall asleep 1,000 times.
2. A bat can hear an insect
   a moving on a tree.
   b flying around in the air.
   c eating a meal.
3. How much does a Kitti's hog-nosed bat weigh?
   a more than other bats
   b the same as other bats
   c the same as a coin
4. Tourists look at the bats in Austin
   a late at night.
   b in the evening.
   c early in the morning.
5. What is Jason planning to do next week?
   a visit a bat farm
   b film bats
   c take photos of bats

Vocabulary

A Complete the words in the sentences.

1. How many days does it take to sail across this o _ _ _ _?
2. To get to the other side of the r _ _ _ _, you have to cross the Simmons Bridge.
3. It's very wet and green in Brazil's beautiful r _ _ _ _ _ _ _ _ _ _.
4. What is the highest m _ _ _ _ _ _ _ in your country?
5. If it stops raining on our planet, all of earth will be a d _ _ _ _ _!
6. My friend Steve and I went fishing at the l _ _ _ near my parents' caravan.

B Choose the correct answers.

1. It's hard to stop environmental pollution, but we must never __ up.
   a dry   b use   c give
2. Orangutans are in danger of dying __ if we don't protect their homes.
   a out   b up   c in
3. Was Jill able to __ to the top of the mountain?
   a keep   b stay   c get
4. Don't leave the water running; __ it off!
   a put   b give   c turn
5. I need to go to the shop because John __ up all the milk.
   a gave   b used   c turned
6. We have to hurry and finish this report; we will soon __ out of time.
   a go   b run   c get

C Complete the text using one word in each gap.

A male leaf-nosed snake found in Madagascar

Madagascar is an island off the southeast coast of Africa, and it's a really amazing place. Over 80% of its plants and animals are found nowhere else on the planet. There are those that live (1) _____ land, such as the flat-tailed gecko. It's a lizard with a tail that looks like a dead leaf. And there are those that live (2) _____ lakes and rivers, such as the Malagasay leaf-nosed snakes, which cannot survive (3) _____ of water. Like the tail of the flat-tailed gecko, this snake's nose also looks a bit like a leaf. Sadly, like so many places on Earth, its plant and animal life is (4) _____ risk of dying out. Many are (5) _____ danger because of the damage that humans do (6) _____ the environment, such as cutting (7) _____ too many trees. Some people in Madagascar have tried to protect a few forests to deal (8) _____ the problem. Still, scientists believe that we are running out of time and that by 2025, many of its rainforests will be gone.

The World Around Us 12

D Complete the words.

  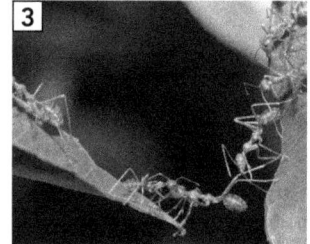 

1 b _ _ _
2 s _ _ _ _ _
3 a _ _ _
4 b _ _ _ _ _ _ _ _ _

   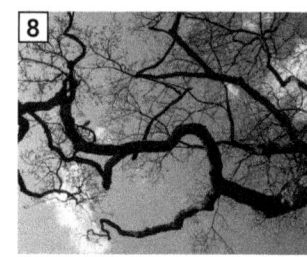

5 f _ _
6 l _ _ _ _ _
7 s _ _ _ _ _
8 b _ _ _ _ _ _ _

E Choose a pet for each of these people.

canary   cat   dog   goldfish   hamster   snake

1 'I want a pet that I can take to the park and go for walks with.'
_____

2 'I'd like to have an animal that will scare all my friends!'
_____

3 'I want an animal that's easy to take care of and lives in water.'
_____

4 'I think I would like a pet that can sing a little song.'
_____

5 'I want a pet that is furry and likes sleeping all day.'
_____

6 'I'd like a pet that I could keep in a cage in my bedroom!'
_____

F Choose the correct answers.

For our class project, we have to (1) ___ vegetables in our garden. It's an excellent idea and it seems quite simple. Just (2) ___ some seeds in the ground and (3) ___ them grow into beautiful plants. (4) ___ them a few times a week, so that they don't dry (5) ___. But what if your garden has (6) ___ that eat the plants? You need to do something to (7) ___ your vegetables. One solution is remove the animals from the plants at night, using the (8) ___ to help you find them. This is better for the (9) ___ than using chemicals to kill them. Follow this advice and you may get some (10) ___ vegetables to eat in the summer!

1	a make	b grow	c plant
2	a plant	b throw	c push
3	a hear	b look	c watch
4	a Wet	b Water	c Dry
5	a down	b of	c up
6	a pandas	b goldfish	c snails
7	a survive	b protect	c search
8	a cages	b volunteers	c moonlight
9	a desert	b environment	c rainforest
10	a massive	b scary	c aggressive

12 The World Around Us

Grammar

Ordering Adjectives; Adjectives ending -ing and -ed

A Circle the correct adjectives.
1. She has a large lovely / wooden table in her living room.
2. It's strange that he's got white garden / modern chairs inside his house.
3. Who's Italian sports / red car is parked in front of the school?
4. These items go in the plastic / small blue bin.
5. She's wearing a comfortable / cotton old sweater.
6. What is this round metal / strange object used for?
7. We went to the new Italian / fantastic restaurant last night.
8. Did you see the beautiful horrible / silk dress Jess was wearing?

B Rewrite the sentences with the adjectives in the correct order.
1. The city is creating a **tea / Japanese / small** garden in our park.
   _____
2. We went to a **rock / crowded / big** concert the other night.
   _____
3. She bought a **metal / bed / used** frame for her bedroom.
   _____
4. They're selling **little / English / tasty** muffins at the street market.
   _____
5. He lives in a **massive / stone / grey** house.
   _____
6. This museum has got **Greek / ancient / beautiful** vases.
   _____
7. The volunteers are planning to clean the **metal / large / dirty** sculpture in front of the cinema.
   _____
8. Can you pass me that **white / plastic / round** plate over there?
   _____

The Japanese Tea Garden in the Golden Gate Park, San Francisco

C Complete the sentences with the adjective form of the words in brackets.
1. This exercise is quite _____ and we're all really _____. Can we stop now? (**tire**)
2. The teacher saw the _____ faces of his students, so he knew the lesson was _____. (**bore**)
3. The audience was quite _____ by the actor's _____ performance. (**amaze**)
4. The radio presenter said some _____ facts about Iceland to his _____ listeners. (**interest**)
5. Lisa and Tom saw a rather _____ film, and they left the cinema feeling quite _____. (**frighten**)
6. The band played their most _____ songs for the very _____ fans. (**excite**)

The World Around Us **12**

D Circle the correct words.

Antarctica is a beautiful but (**1**) frightened / frighten / frightening place, especially in the summer. It's scary to think, but from the end of March until September, the sun does not appear in the sky. That's six months of almost complete darkness! It means if you're a scientist who is (**2**) interested / interest / interesting in studying this continent, it's best to wait until autumn to go there. Getting around Antarctica is a very (**3**) tiring / tire / tired experience. There are few roads and they are usually covered in snow. This makes it very difficult to explore. But those who travel there say Antarctica is an (**4**) excited / exciting / excite place that's full of adventure. The bright white snow and deep blue ocean (**5**) amazed / amaze / amazing everyone who makes the journey to see it. Of course, there are no cities in Antarctica, so if you're looking for entertainment, you might feel a bit (**6**) bore / bored / boring.

Two men travelling through icy surroundings in Antarctica

Listening

A Read the *Exam Reminder*. What should you do the second time you hear the recording?

_____

B 12.1 Listen and complete the *Exam Task*.

Exam Task

Listen to Jessica talking to her classmate Jorge about his home country. For each question, choose the right answer (**a**, **b** or **c**). You will hear the conversation twice.

1 When did Jorge last visit his home country?
  a spring
  b summer
  c autumn
2 What does Jorge miss about Spain?
  a swimming
  b the warm weather
  c not having rain
3 How long did it take Jorge to get to his local beach?
  a ten minutes
  b twenty minutes
  c one hour
4 What does Jorge say is tiring?
  a windsurfing
  b bird watching
  c bike riding
5 Which animal does Jorge say is in danger?
  a a type of turtle
  b a type of horse
  c a type of cat

Exam Reminder

Preparing to choose the right option
- Look at each answer option before you listen to the recording and think about what the speakers might say to each other if this was the right answer.
- Remember to think about the different ways the speakers might talk about numbers, rules and times.
- Remember that when you listen to the recording the second time, you should check your answers.

C 12.2 Listen again and check your answers.

Writing: a report

Learning Reminder

Structuring a report
- Remember to use these section headings when you write a report: Introduction, Background, Findings, Conclusion / Recommendations.
- Make sure you use formal vocabulary and structures when you write a report. Remember to use full forms rather than contractions.

A Complete the sentences from reports with these words.

based   caused   purpose   suggest   would

1 The pollution is _____ by chemicals in the river.
2 I _____ that we switch off the lights at night.
3 The _____ of this report is to discuss how we can prevent the extinction of endangered species.
4 It _____ be a good idea to recycle more paper.
5 The results are _____ on information given by the students.

B Read the email and the notes and circle the correct words.

Email Message

Dear Mr Jones,
I'm writing a report on recycling at school for the class project you gave us. I've sent questionnaires to the students in my class and to the head teacher, and I've already found out some interesting information. I'm surprised that the school doesn't recycle plastic! I'll send you my report when I've finished it.
Best wishes,
Richard

Questionnaire information
- no recycling bins in classrooms - students want bins in classrooms
- need to buy more recycled paper - school only buys 20%
- school canteen buys a lot of plastic drinks bottles - replace with recyclable glass bottles

1 Richard is a teacher / student.
2 Richard is going to write a report / an email.
3 Richard / Mr Jones is doing a project about recycling.

C Read the example report and circle the correct words.

(1) Findings / Introduction
The purpose of this report is to make suggestions about how our school can recycle more. It is based on results from a questionnaire I gave to students and the head teacher.

(2) Introduction / Background
We are harming the environment by cutting down trees to make paper and by the processes needed to make plastic and glass, so we need to recycle more.

(3) Findings / Conclusion
- Only 20% of the paper the school buys is recycled paper.
- The school does not recycle plastic.
- The school canteen buys too many plastic drinks bottles.

(4) Background / Conclusion
The school can do more to help the environment through recycling. I recommend they:
- put recycling bins into the classrooms.
- find recycling bins in the city where we can take used plastic.
- buy more recycled paper.
- replace the plastic drinks bottles with recyclable glass bottles.

If the information you're looking for isn't in the first text, try to find it in the other text.

D Read and complete the *Exam Task* below. Don't forget to use the *Useful Expressions* on page 157 of your Student's Book.

Exam Task

Read the email and the notes. Fill in the information in Pedro's report

Information from questionnaire
- need to encourage more animals, insects and birds into garden - make pond for drinking and bathing
- need to build places animals and insects can live over winter - branches in corner
- provide food for animals - plant fruit bushes, put bird food in bird feeders

Email Message

Hi Sally,
I want to set up an area in the school's garden for wildlife, so I've sent questionnaires to the students and the staff at a local wildlife centre to find out what we should do. Did you know that it's important to feed the birds in the summer as well as the winter? If you are interested in helping, I can send you the report when I've written it.
Pedro

Introduction
The purpose of this report is to propose ideas for the school's wildlife garden. It is based on the results of a questionnaire I gave to the school's students and staff at the local (1) _____ centre.

Background
A lot of animals, birds and insects in our country are at risk of being endangered, so we need to encourage them into our garden.

Findings
- Providing places for wildlife to (2) _____ and bathe would encourage them into the garden.
- Many insects and animals need places to live in winter.
- Wildlife often can't find enough food.

Recommendations
We can do more to encourage wildlife. I recommend we:
- build a (3) _____ to give wildlife somewhere to drink and bathe.
- put tree (4) _____ in the corner to give wildlife a place to live in winter.
- plant fruit bushes and put food in the bird feeders even in (5) _____

Review 6

Vocabulary

A Choose the correct answers.

1 'Do I need to bring my umbrella?'
   'No, it's quite ___ at the moment.'
   a sunny   c snowy
   b rainy   d icy

2 The hills were covered in ___ and you could hardly see them.
   a storms   c rain
   b wind   d fog

3 Paul wore a very heavy coat because it was ___ outside.
   a cool   c warm
   b boiling   d freezing

4 '___ the weather like today?'
   'Warm and beautiful, as always!'
   a When's   c How's
   b Where's   d What's

5 The boats in Thailand didn't go out to sea because it was very ___.
   a snowy   c stormy
   b icy   d sunny

6 'When is your cousin's birthday?'
   'It's in ___. It's on the 4th of April.'
   a summer   c winter
   b spring   d autumn

7 Did you see that ___ in the sky last night?
   a flood   c thunder
   b lightning   d bush fire

8 The plants are slowly dying because of the terrible ___.
   a fire   c drought
   b storm   d flood

9 'What's your favourite season?'
   'It's ___ because that's when the leaves change colour on the trees.'
   a autumn   c spring
   b summer   d winter

10 It's getting cold. Should we turn the ___ on?
   a bush fire   c heater
   b sunshine   d boiling

11 Shall we take a boat out on the ___ this weekend?'
   a lake   c desert
   b rainforest   d mountain

12 We have to do something about climate change, but we're ___ out of time.
   a getting   c running
   b taking   d going

13 We will soon ___ up the world's supply of fossil fuels.
   a pick   c use
   b take   d do

14 There's a lovely ___ that flows through the centre of town.
   a lake   c ocean
   b sea   d river

15 Yesterday, Sarah fell over and ___ her foot badly.
   a injured   c collapsed
   b buried   d stung

16 To start a garden, you must first ___ some seeds.
   a grow   c plant
   b make   d put

17 Don't hit the ___ of that tree – it will break.
   a plant   c branch
   b ground   d leaf

18 I think ___ make the best pets.
   a flies   c snails
   b ants   d cats

19 'What sort of pet needs a cage?'
   'I think ___ definitely do.'
   a cats   c goldfish
   b dogs   d canaries

20 ___ are useful because they can make honey.
   a Flies   c Butterflies
   b Bees   d Spiders

Grammar

B Choose the correct answers.

1 Brazil is definitely ___ than the UK.
  a the warmest   c warm
  b warmest   d warmer

2 'I don't like Tom's new hairstyle.'
  'Yes, it looks ___ than before.'
  a badly   c bad
  b worst   d worse

3 I think this summer has been ___ wetter than last summer.
  a more   c –
  b most   d very

4 'It takes a long time to get to Uncle Terry's house.'
  'Oh, it's not ___ far as you think.'
  a very   c more
  b so   d most

5 I can do my maths homework ___ than my English homework.
  a as easy as   c more easy
  b as easily as d more easily

6 Eating junk food all day is the ___ thing you can do to your body.
  a worst   c bad
  b badly   d worse

7 'How was your hiking trip?'
  'It was the ___ holiday I've had in a while!'
  a better   c well
  b good   d best

8 It snowed the ___ during the afternoon.
  a more heavy   c most heavily
  b more heavily   d most heavy

9 'What's the ___ mountain in the world?'
  'Mount Everest, of course.'
  a most highly   c higher
  b high   d highest

10 That was the ___ dangerous storm we've had all year.
  a too   c most
  b more   d –

11 'What did you get at the book shop?'
   'I got a(n) ___ book.'
   a Italian used grammar   c used Italian grammar
   b grammar Italian used   d Italian grammar used

12 That's a ___ sweater you're wearing.
   a lovely red cotton   c cotton lovely red
   b red cotton lovely   d lovely cotton red

13 I need a ___ object for my art project.
   a metal long round   c round metal long
   b long round metal   d metal round long

14 She lives on a ___ boat in the summer.
   a wooden tiny house   c tiny wooden house
   b tiny house wooden   d wooden house tiny

15 They're finally closing down that ___ factory on the edge of town.
   a shoe polluted ugly   c ugly polluted shoe
   b ugly shoe polluted   d polluted ugly shoe

16 'What is Helen going to study at university?'
   'She's very ___ in marine biology.'
   a interest   c interesting
   b interestingly   d interested

17 I don't want to see a horror film. They're ___!
   a fright   c frighten
   b frightening   d frightened

18 If you think painting is ___, why do you do it?
   a boredom   c bored
   b bore   d boring

19 I'm ___ that people still throw rubbish onto the streets.
   a amazed   c amaze
   b amazing   d amazingly

20 Michelle passed her history exam, which was ___ news.
   a surprisingly   c surprised
   b surprising   d surprise

www.ingramcontent.com/pod-product-compliance
Ingram Content Group UK Ltd.
Pitfield, Milton Keynes, MK11 3LW, UK
UKHW060159240426
12048UKWH00028B/1663